TRADITIONAL NEEDLE ARTS

EMBROIDERY

TRADITIONAL NEEDLE ARTS

EMBROIDERY

25 classic step-by-step projects

KATRIN CARGILL

PHOTOGRAPHY BY DAVID MONTGOMERY

MITCHELL BEAZLEY

To my sisters Christeli and Andrea, with love and laughter

First published in Great Britain in 1995
by Mitchell Beazley
an imprint of Reed Consumer Books Limited
Michelin House, 81 Fulham Road, London SW3 6RB
and Auckland, Melbourne, Singapore and Toronto

Art Director	JACQUI SMALL
Executive Editor	JUDITH MORE
Executive Art Editor	LARRAINE SHAMWANA
Editors	MARGOT RICHARDSON & JULIA NORTH
Production	MICHELLE THOMAS
Design	INGUNN CECILIE JENSEN
Stylist	KATRIN CARGILL
Photographer	DAVID MONTGOMERY
Illustrator	AMANDA PATTON

A CIP record for this book is available from the British Library

ISBN 1 85732 567 2

The publishers have made every effort to ensure that all
instructions given in this book are accurate and safe but they
cannot accept liability for any resulting injury, damage or loss to
either person or property, whether direct or consequential and
howsoever arising.
The colours in the keys and charts in this book are as near to the
true colour of the yarns as possible, but some variation may occur.
The author and publishers will be grateful for any information
which will assist them in keeping future editions up to date.

Typeset in Perpetua 12/16 and 10/12pt
Index compiled by Hilary Bird
Printed and bound in Barcelona, Spain by Cayfosa

Contents

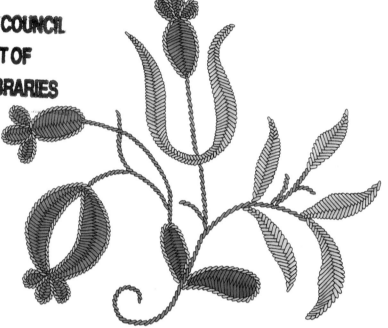

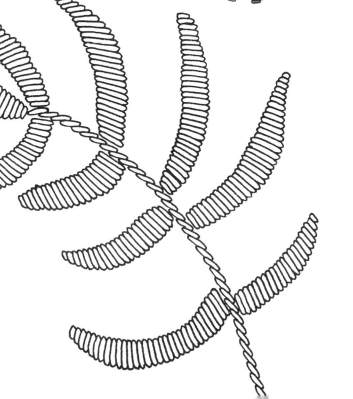

Introduction

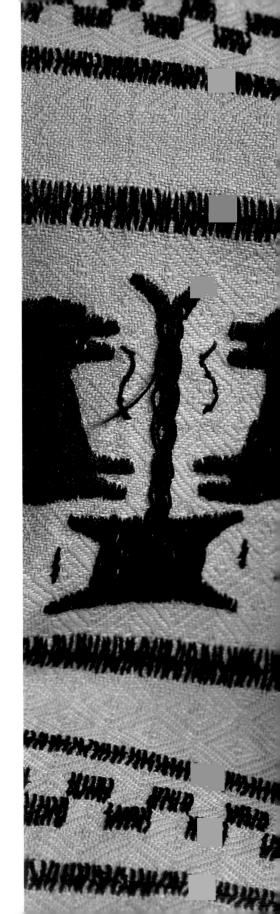

With the fast-paced lives we lead today there is a craving for a return to home-made crafts, a yearning to work with one's hands and to derive satisfaction from creating something attractive. In the past, learning to embroider and sew was a highly important part of a young woman's education. With the advent of machinery and the liberated woman, needlework has – for many people – become no more than a distant memory. Now, however, there is a revival of these crafts coupled with the desire to have a pastime that counteracts the pace of modern life.

Embroidery, the embellishment of fabric with the use of needle and thread, has been practised for thousands of years. As early as clothing was worn, embroidery was used to decorate garments with designs rooted in ancient superstitions and activities of daily life.

The earliest form of embroidery was actually copied from body tattoos. Remains of heavily tattooed bodies – from which designs have been adapted to embroidery – have been found as far afield as Zaire and Siberia. In fact, embroidery is more closely linked to tattooing than weaving or knitting, as both tattooing and embroidery used symbolism transformed into pattern.

The hunting of animals was often a basis for primitive cults and subsequently gave rise to forms and images translated into embroidery. The hunted animals, such as wolves, wild boar or fowl were frequently shown in stylized and repetitive patterns. Similarly, weapons and protective clothing evolved into rows of repeated patterns. Pagan symbolism was depicted in a multitude of forms including stars, crosses, zig-zags, waves, spirals, plants, flowers and different animals.

RIGHT The hunting of animals gave rise to forms and images that were eventually translated into embroidery, as can be seen on this detail of a fringed runner. Wolves, wild boar or fowl were often shown as part of a stylized and repetitive pattern.

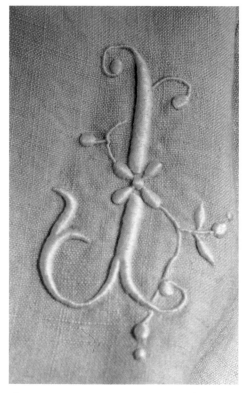

FAR RIGHT AND ABOVE Monograms, also known as ciphers, were originally used on letters and seals, but later became common as an identification on household linens and clothing.

These symbols have been absorbed and assimilated, and are still to be found in modern embroidery.

Almost universally, embroidery represented something of significance about the wearer or the owner. Embroidery served as a means of identifying what village or tribe a person belonged to, whether they were married, had children, or what their social class was. Important events such as birth, marriage and even death were celebrated with significant pieces of embroidery. Household goods were commonly stitched to form part of a wedding trousseau.

With the advent of widespread non-pagan religions – such as Buddhism, Christianity, Hinduism and Islam – more modern symbols, specific to the religion, came into being. However, like the motifs of pagan cultures, the symbols used in the embroidery of Eastern religions and Christianity were often derived from the common world of nature. Although the Islamic holy book, the Qur'an, forbids the depiction of living forms, we still see geometric and stylized forms in Islamic embroidery that bear some resemblance to the animals and plants which inspired them. Generally, in Eastern cultures, embroidery has remained closer to its origins than in the West, where embroidery has become a more individualized art form subject to many artistic influences.

Embroidered garments are seen on Greek vases of the 6th and 7th century BC, but the earliest known examples of embroidery belong to the Scythians, horsemen who inhabited the Steppes, and date back to the 3rd and 5th centuries BC. The ancient city of Byzantium, present-day Istanbul, produced embroideries decadently woven with gold from AD330 until the 15th century.

RIGHT Classical designs were often based on nature, such as the Greek laurel wreath on this handkerchief, and had a long-lasting influence on the motifs used for embroidery.

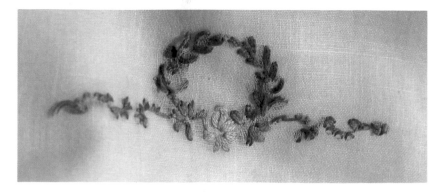

ABOVE Samplers became popular in England, and later America, in the 16th century. This detail from a house-sampler shows a wide variety of embroidery stitches.

BELOW Designs based on the "tree of life" motif – seen in early Indian embroidery – are still commonly found today.

Other Eastern examples of embroidery are the Chinese Imperial silk robes of the Manchu dynasty, dating back to the 17th century, and numerous pieces created in India during the Mughal period – from 1556 – which were shipped to Europe through the East India trade. A flowering-tree motif, used extensively in this genre of Indian embroidery, had a particularly strong influence on English embroidery, and is still commonly used today.

Northern European embroidery was dominated by ecclesiastical and, to a lesser extent, historical depictions, until the time of the Renaissance. A 10th-century stole belonging to St Cuthbert, which had been embroidered in gold thread, is perhaps the earliest example of English embroidery. The 11th-century Bayeux tapestry, an historical depiction of the Norman conquest, is one of the largest and earliest secular examples of embroidery still preserved in its entirety. England's most renowned and prolific period of embroidery, from 1100 to 1350, is known throughout Europe as "Englishwork". During the 16th century in Western Europe, the art of embroidery moved away from the professional sphere and into that of the amateur craftsperson.

As people became more wealthy, the privileged classes would patronize an embroiderer. Embroidery also became a pastime for ladies of leisure. Whitework, white stitching on white cloth, was a popular form of embroidery, and was used extensively throughout Europe, from the 16th century onward. Garments as well as church, table linen and bed linen were decorated, and it was normally used in conjunction with lace. The fashion for crewel work in 16th-century England was reflected in the embroidery of 17th and 18th-century North America. Samplers became very popular in England, and later in America. They fulfilled several functions: they served as a record of stitches and designs, a testbed for new stitches and motifs, and also provided a means of highlighting the ability and diversity of the needlewoman. By the end of the 18th century, samplers began to be worked to commemorate particular events – coronations for example. Today, however, they can be viewed as purely decorative pieces in their own right. At a similar time, some of the native American tribes developed a type of embroidery known as quill work. This essentially involved the embroidering of animal skins or bark with different coloured porcupine quills. Thus, in the same country and during the same era, there were two highly diverse methods of embroidery – one a single native tradition, and the other a descendant of many different cultures and ways.

The transmission of ideas, symbols and patterns in embroidery has been facilitated by the fact that cloth and garments are traded, bought and sold across the world. The original meanings of the symbols may have been lost, but the symbols themselves have remained. For example, pieces from Salamanca in Spain are not embroidered with images of local animals, but instead depict scenes such as those found on early cave paintings and the embroidery of the Scythians. As many embroidery motifs are based on organic forms found in variation throughout the world, so the process of interchanging and accepting of symbols and designs from diverse and far-away cultures becomes much easier.

ABOVE The original meanings of symbols used in embroidery have often been lost, but the symbols themselves, like this floral/sun motif, have remained.

BELOW Many embroidered motifs are based on organic forms. Designs range from the naturalistic, like this flower sprig, to the stylized, like the motif above.

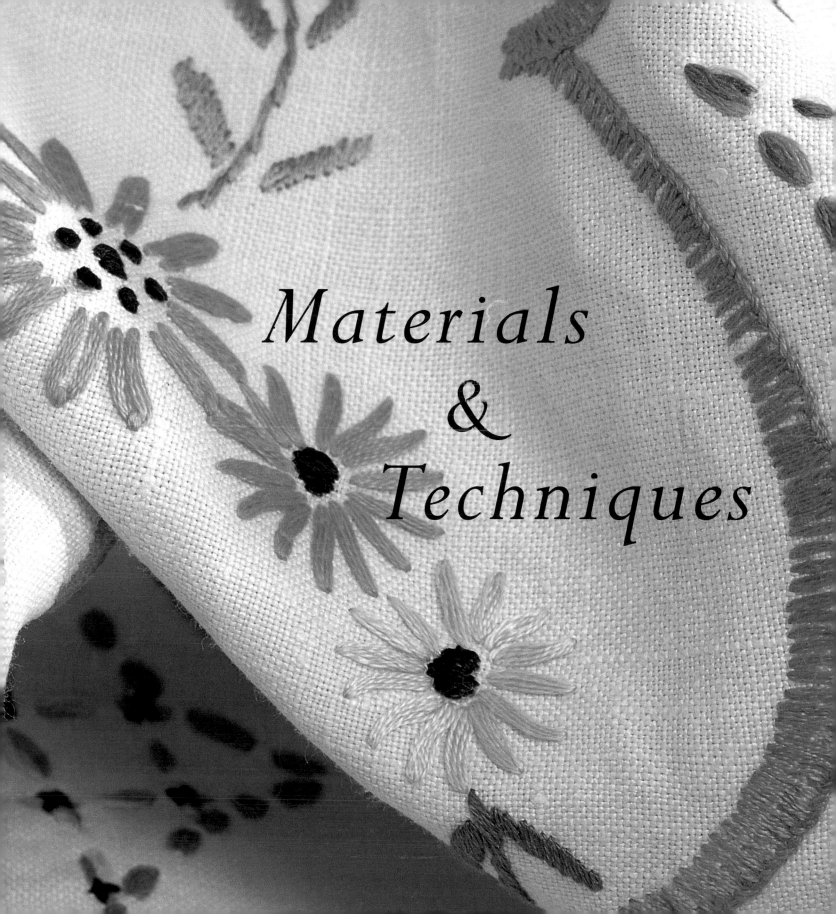

Materials
&
Techniques

Before you begin

The projects that are included in this book are all based on real items of needlework, some of which are valuable antiques. There is something to suit every ability, from simple projects for the beginner (such as the hand towel on page 102, or the tray cloth on page 54), to more complicated pieces for the advanced needlewoman (the Peacock tablecloth on page 49). The simple items essentially require the application of time and a bit of planning. They make particularly good projects for youngsters starting out in embroidery. Embroidered gifts always make welcome surprises, especially if they are in some way personalised with the recipient's initials, and a useful alphabet is included for this purpose (page 88).

For all the projects in the book, some basic rules and requirements apply. You will also find descriptions and illustrations of all the stitches you may encounter in the book (see page 18).

BASIC EMBROIDERERS' REQUIREMENTS
These include:
• Fabric, thread, needle.
• Embroidery hoops or frame.
• Dressmaking carbon/transfer paper.
• Dressmaker's marking pencils.
• Embroidery scissors.
• Good light source.
• Clean and dry hands.

FABRICS FOR EMBROIDERY
Almost any material can be embroidered, but all the items in this book were made from different types of linen and cotton. Linen is particularly well suited to embroidered pieces as it usually has equal numbers of threads in each direction (warp and weft). This type of fabric is referred to as even weave. It makes the plotting of the pattern much easier, as well as making the stitches even in all directions and minimizing distortion and pulling. Linen also launders well, looking like new time and time again, so it is especially suited to items like tablecloths that will be frequently laundered.

EMBROIDERY THREADS AND FLOSSES
There are many types of embroidery threads: from silks to synthetics, linens, cottons and wools. For the majority of the projects in this book, stranded cotton has been specified: it is the most common and versatile of embroidery threads, and there is a wide selection of colours. It consists

LEFT A cotton hand towel, as seen here, can be effectively embellished with hand embroidery.

of six strands which can be used complete but are more commonly divided into one to four strands. The colours are listed with each project for both DMC and Anchor brands. Coton Perlé (pearl cotton) has been specified for the Curved Floral Tie-back (on page 100). It is twisted and has a sheen, and is available in many weights and colours. An alternative thread that you may wish to use for some projects is Filo Floss, a six-stranded plied silk with a rich sheen which, like stranded cotton, is mostly divided into one or two strands for finer work. Crewel wool, a fine yet strong 2-ply wool, is suggested for the Crewel Wallhanging on page 32.

NEEDLES

It is important to use the right type of needle for embroidering. They vary from being quite blunt, for use on canvas work and counted linen work, to very fine and sharp for fine cottons and silks. There are varying sizes: the higher the size number, the smaller the hole. A general rule of thumb is to use a hole through which the thread passes easily.

The most common embroidery needle is called a crewel needle. This is a sharp, long and slim needle that passes easily through most fabrics. If the fabric shows large holes, use a finer needle. For each project in the book we specify the recommended needle size.

EMBROIDERY FRAMES

There are no hard and fast rules about using frames for embroidery. Some people find it easier to work the fabric in their hands, while others prefer a frame in which

the fabric is held taught and even, especially for finer work. There are many types of frames on the market, but the most common are the hoop or the slate frame. The choices are entirely personal and, as you become more proficient, you can of course experiment with the different types.

TRANSFERRING THE DESIGN

For each project we include a line drawing of the pattern. Parts of the design that are repeated have been indicated, and there is an overall plan of how it is used on the finished object. The various areas are marked for size. In cases where they are too big for the book they are reduced in scale. To enlarge them to the right size, transfer the pattern onto graph paper and increase the proportion to the desired size; or use a photocopier to enlarge them. Some patterns are actual size and can be traced directly onto tracing or transfer paper.

With counted-thread work (such as the Geometric and Heart-motif cushions), putting the design onto fabric is fairly straightforward. Always cut a piece of cloth slightly

larger than required (as specified in each project). Iron it flat and fold it in half vertically. Using an ordinary running or tacking stitch, sew a line down the middle. Repeat this for a horizontal line, also along the middle. This will be your main guide for plotting the pattern. Where patterns are repeated with a "mirror" image, use the same logical folding method to plot out the various repeats. Remember always to work from the centre outward, so you don't find that you suddenly run out of fabric.

There are various other methods for transferring designs onto fabric. The most useful to know for the projects within this book are the running stitch method and the transfer method.

The running stitch method works well for both smooth and more textured fabrics. First, trace the design onto tracing paper. Then cut a piece of fabric slightly larger than required and iron flat. Work horizontal and vertical lines of tacking stitches through the centre of the area to be used. Cut a piece of tracing paper to match and trace the design onto it. Rule horizontal and vertical lines through the centre of the design. Place the tracing on the right side of the material, matching the centre lines, and pin together. Use a colour thread which will show up on the fabric and work running stitches along all of the pattern, being careful to follow the design accurately. For curves and more complex shapes, make the stitches smaller or you will lose the pattern when it comes to embroidering. For straight lines, the stitches can be larger. Remember always to secure the beginnings and ends with back stitches. Once you have finished tracing, lay the whole thing on a flat surface and gently tear away the tracing paper. Begin the embroidery and remove the running stitches as you progress.

For very fine patterns (such as the Curved Floral Tie-back on page 100) you might find it better to use dressmaker's carbon or transfer paper rather than running stitches. This is a non-smudge carbon paper – generally available at haberdashery shops – and comes in several colours. It is not effective on heavily textured fabrics. Choose one that contrasts best with the colour of your fabric. Follow all the steps for the running stitch method up until attaching it to the fabric. Place the fabric right side up on a hard surface, and place the transfer paper, shiny side down, on the fabric. Place the tracing paper over this, remembering to match the centre lines. Pin the tracing paper and fabric together, and trace over the design with a ballpoint pen or a pencil. Remove the transfer and tracing paper very carefully, and begin the embroidery. Make sure that the stitches extend slightly beyond the carbon paper lines, so that they do not show when the embroidery is finished.

LEFT Hoops and frames can assist the embroiderer.
BELOW A piece in progress, showing the transfer method.

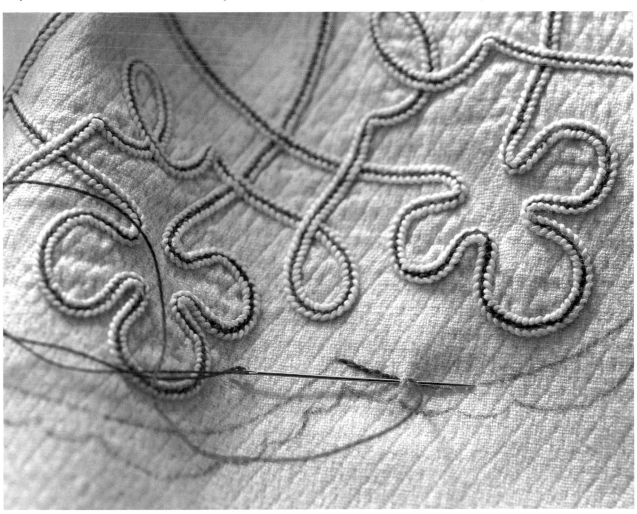

BACK STITCH

Bring the needle through the fabric, from the wrong side to the right, at A. Insert the needle at B, and come out again at C. Insert the needle again at A, and go an equal distance further on, past C. Repeat in this way until you have the desired number of stitches.

STEM STITCH

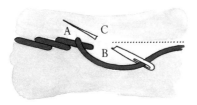

This stitch is like backstitch, but the stitches overlap each other, giving a rope-like effect. Bring the needle through the fabric, from the wrong side to the right, at A. Insert the needle at B, and come out again at C, half-way back. Repeat, always keeping the thread on the same side of the needle.

SPLIT STITCH

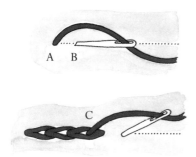

This is like stem stitch, but the thread is split half-way along the stitch. Bring the needle through the fabric, from the wrong side to the right, at A. Insert the needle at B, and come out again at C, half-way back inside the stitch. Repeat.

CORAL STITCH

Work from right to left. Bring the thread through to the right side of the fabric. Then, slightly to the left, make a small vertical stitch. (Make sure that the thread passes under the point of the needle from left to right.) Finally, pull gently to the left to form a knot.

SATIN STITCH

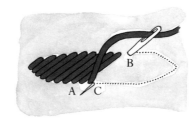

For this filling stitch, place straight stitches close together. Bring the needle through the fabric, from the wrong side to the right, at A. Insert the needle at B, and come out again at C, as close as possible to A. Repeat. It is important to keep the stitches neat and smooth.

CROSS STITCH

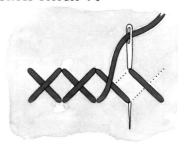

If possible, it is a good idea to work cross stitches in a line, first stitching half the crosses, and then coming back along the line to complete them. However you choose to work, it is essential that the top stitches of the cross all slant in the same direction. Repeat this process for the subsequent stitches.

HALF-CROSS STITCH

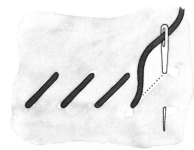

Work one line of stitches, as shown above: bring the needle through the fabric, from the wrong side to the right, at point A. Insert the needle at B, and come out again at C. Half-cross stitches should be placed quite close together, as in tapestry work.

HERRINGBONE STITCH

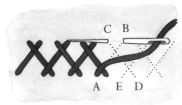

This is a variation of cross stitch, where the threads overlap at their ends, rather than in the centre. Bring the needle through the fabric at A and insert it at B, coming out again at C. From there go to D, and come out again at E. Repeat.

FISHBONE STITCH

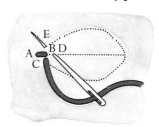

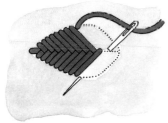

In this densely packed stitch of the cross stitch family the centre ends of the stitches overlap. It is particularly effective for creating leaves. Bring the needle through the fabric at A (the tip of the leaf) and insert it at B. Then go to C, and come out again at D (just below B). Then go to the other side of the leaf at E. Continue in this way, alternating between each side of the leaf and following the outline shape.

BLANKET STITCH

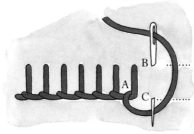

Often used to finish edges, especially on blankets (hence the name). Bring the needle through the fabric at A. Insert the needle at B and come out again at C, looping the thread under the needle before pulling it tight. Repeat. The arms of the blanket stitches can be stitched in varying lengths for a decorative effect.

BUTTONHOLE STITCH

This is worked in exactly the same way as blanket stitch, except that the stitches are placed as close together as possible, to form a firm edging. It is also possible to work it in a circle, to create decorative spheres that look like flowers.

CHAIN STITCH

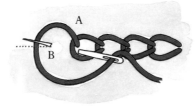

Either use this for outlining, or for filling areas if you work stitches very closely together. Bring the needle through the fabric at A. Insert it again at A and come out at B, looping the thread under the needle before pulling it through. To make the next stitch, insert the needle

again at B, come out as before; loop the thread under the needle before pulling it through. Repeat.

LAZY-DAISY STITCH

This variation of chain stitch makes a pretty flower. Eight chain stitches, anchored at their outer end, are worked around a central point. Bring the needle through the fabric at A. Insert it again at A and come out again at B, looping the thread under the needle before pulling it through. To anchor the stitch, insert the needle at C, and move onto the next stitch. Repeat.

FRENCH KNOTS

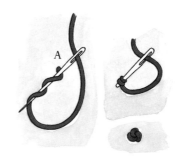

These create a raised, textured effect. Bring the needle through the fabric at A. Holding the thread taut with one hand, wind it around the needle twice, and reinsert the needle near to point A, keeping the thread taut as you pull the needle through.

BULLION KNOTS

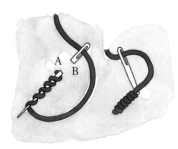

These are similar to French knots, except that they create a larger stitch. Bring the needle through the fabric at A. Insert it at B, and bring it up again at A, but leave the needle in the fabric as shown. Wind the thread around the needle five or six times, then pull the needle gently through the fabric and the wound thread, toward B. Pull the thread tight, using the needle to pack the wound thread together if necessary. Insert needle again into B.

FEATHER STITCH

This is a looped stitch, a little like chain stitch, that has stitches alternating to either side of a central line. Bring the needle through the fabric at A. Then insert it at B and come out again at C, looping the thread under the needle before pulling it through. Then insert the needle at D, and come out again at E, looping the thread under the needle before pulling it through. Repeat this, alternating from side to side.

FOUR-SIDED STITCH

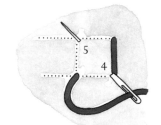

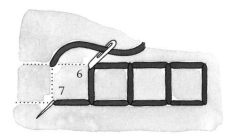

This is always worked in horizontal rows, running with the grain of the fabric, and moving from right to left. Follow the numbered points illustrated above, and always pull each stitch tight. When you come to the end of a row, turn the fabric upside-down. You should then work the next row in the same way as the first.

FINISHING TOUCHES
SLIP STITCH

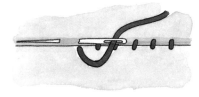

This stitch is used for an almost invisible finish on hems. First, slide the needle through the folded edge and at the same place, pick up a thread of the under-fabric. Then continue, spacing stitches 3–6 mm (⅛–¼in apart).

HEM STITCH

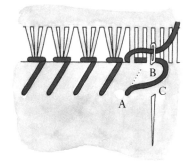

A decorative method of anchoring a hem, using drawn threads.

1 Pull out two or three threads along the stitching line. Turn the hem up to the edge of the drawn threads.

2 Bring the needle through at A, through the hem. Take the thread to the right, then pointing the needle toward the left, pass it under and over two or three fabric threads (use the same number each time). Pull through and, with the needle perpendicular, insert at B and bring through to the front of the material at C, on a line where the thread first came up. Repeat.

HOW TO MITRE A CORNER

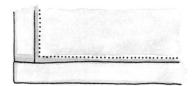

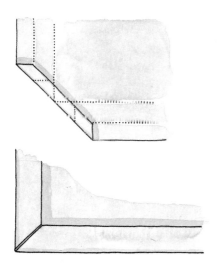

1 On each raw edge, turn over a small amount of fabric, wrong sides together. (Exact measurements are given for each project.) Press. Turn over a slightly larger amount and press well, especially at the corners. Pin the hem to within 7.5 cm/3in of each corner.

2 Unfold each corner, and fold the corner of the fabric up so that there is an exact diagonal at the point of the corner. Press. Unfold and trim the fabric near the diagonal fold.

3 Turn the diagonal over along the pressed line, then fold each side back up along its pressing lines to form a neat mitred corner. Pin in place, then slipstitch the hem.

ABOVE The type of thread used in embroidery can create many different looks, from heavy crewel wool which gives a a thick matt finish, to fine glossy silk which can be used in different thicknesses. A selection is shown here. From top to bottom: Crewel wool, stranded silk floss, artificial stranded silk floss, stranded cotton and cotton pearl.

Samplers

Stumpwork picture

Raised or embossed embroidery, also known as stumpwork, is a charming form of stitchery which depicts events and happenings, often in three dimensions, by the use of padded and raised shapes. It also combines many types of stitches and even some needlelace to create various textures. Its peak of popularity in England lasted for a relatively short period of time – from approximately 1640 to 1680.

Surviving examples of stumpwork depict both biblical and general day-to-day events. The images or figures were often made up individually, then attached to the main piece of fabric. Bound wire and vellum were frequently used to form shapes, as were a variety of other materials such as real hair, beads, metallic threads, and feathers. It is a highly charming and naïve form of embroidery which seems to be gaining in popularity again, largely due to its use of different characters and "real" events, as well as the use of free-form interpretations.

This particular piece portrays a man and a woman, surrounded by flowers with a large bird and a butterfly. The raised clothing of the couple was made from individual pieces of needlelace, but because it is quite complicated to create, directions given here suggest scraps of fabric and lace to create the figures' clothing, feet and hands.

RIGHT Use leftover scraps of material and lace, combined with embroidery, to recreate this charming picture of a 17th-century lady and gentleman.
ABOVE The woman's body is slightly raised from the embroidery's surface.

ABILITY LEVEL: Intermediate

SIZE OF FINISHED STITCHED AREA:
34 x 20 cm/13½ x 8in

STRANDED COTTON/EMBROIDERY FLOSS:
4 strands

NEEDLE SIZE: 5

FABRIC:
45 x 30 cm/18 x 12in heavy cotton or linen. Scraps of coloured fabric for clothes and grounds on which the figures stand (to match or tone in with embroidery thread or floss used on the background).

Coarse cotton lace for collars. Felt and/or cotton wool for padding.

TO EMBROIDER AND MAKE UP
1 Cut out the clothing shapes shown overleaf.

2 Slipstitch the shapes down in place, turning the edges under and

tucking in bits of soft filling as you go. This may involve some experimentation to get the relative prominence of the shapes correct. Start with the green rectangles, then work up through the feet and clothes, overlapping pieces as necessary; stitch down the hands, then lap the sleeves over them.

Finish by attaching the lace collars, making their upper edges as neat as possible, as there will be nothing to overlap over the top of them.

3 Finally, embroider the faces and hair, the detail on the front of the woman's skirt, and also the background features.

COLOURS AND STITCHES:

					DMC	Anchor
	⋀	○			434	370
	⍀	⋀	⍀⍀		783	307
	⍀	⍀	⋀	○	3032	903
	⋀	⍀⍀			414	235
	⍀	⍀⍀	○	𝒞	317	233
	⍀	⋀	⋀	○	926	838
	⍀⍀				523	858

27

MAN

The outlines of the shapes below represent the "sewing" line. You should allow an extra 5 mm/¼in when cutting out. Cutting notches around the corners of each piece will help you to fold in the edges of the fabric.

NOTE: The templates below are actual size, but the patterns shown on the previous pages need to be enlarged to 127%.

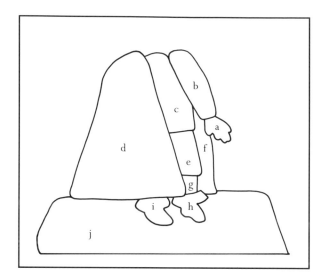

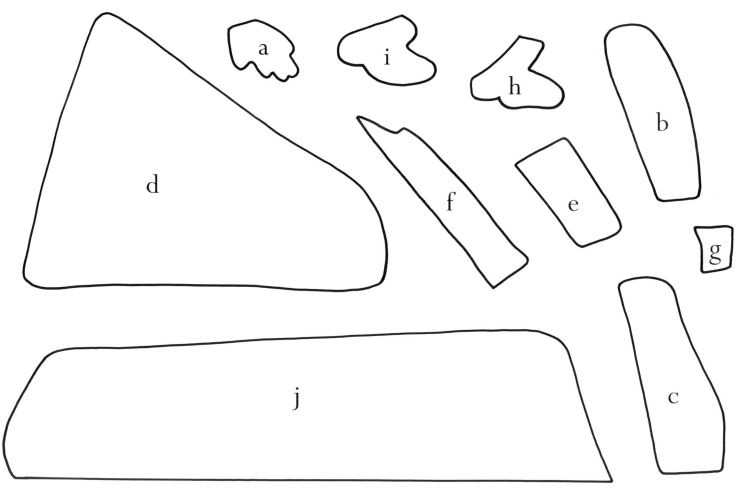

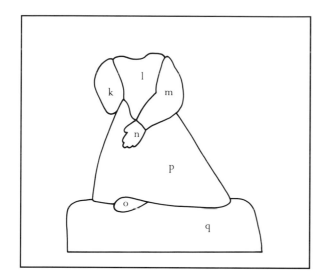

WOMAN

Follow the same directions as for the male figure opposite.

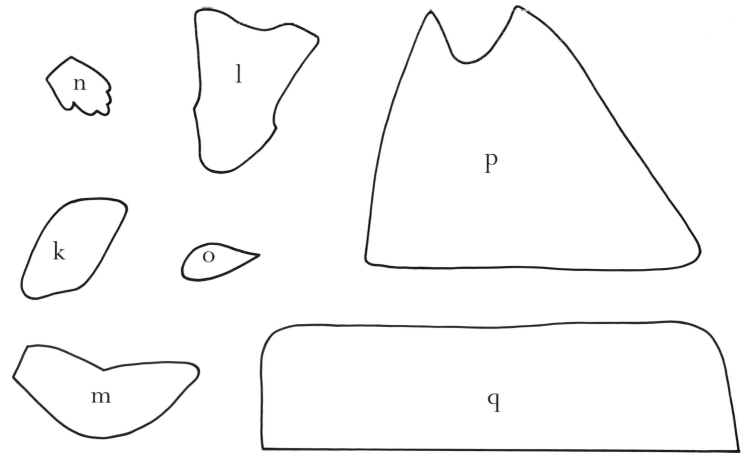

Carnation sampler

The carnation, a symbol of fertility, was widely used as a motif on garments (especially wedding gowns) and household goods. This naïve sampler, stitched onto a heavy, hand-loomed linen, comes from part of an antique Eastern European altar cloth which had been damaged. The simple pattern of the pair of urns with carnation plants, set over a decorative border, is fairly simple to stitch. Using an even-weave linen as the background cloth makes the plotting of the design easier than other materials. The piece could be personalized by stitching names or a date over the top of the carnations.

Stitches used on this sampler include cross stitch, half-cross stitch and back stitch. If you are new to embroidery, this is a good simple piece on which to practise these stitches.

ABILITY LEVEL: Intermediate

SIZE OF FINISHED STITCHED AREA: 193 x 190 mm/7⅝ x 7½in (enlarge patterns to 110%).

DIMENSIONS OF ONE CARNATION:
180 x 90 mm/7 x 3½in

WIDTH OF BORDER:
14 mm/⁹⁄₁₆in

STRANDED COTTON/ EMBROIDERY FLOSS: 2 strands

NEEDLE SIZE: 8

FABRIC:
30 x 30 cm/12 x 12in fine cream linen, or Zweigart 36-count Edinborough 3217 (Linen, Col no 222), or Charles Craft 32-count Real Irish Linen (Col "Cream")

COLOURS AND STITCHES:

		DMC	Anchor
	ℒ ✕	310	403
	ℒ ✕	518	168
	ℒ ✕	312	979
	ℒ	733	280
	ℒ ✕	937	268
	ℒ	356	5975

		DMC	Anchor
	ℒ ✕	834	874
	ℒ ✕ ℒ	3712	9
	ℒ ✕	350	11

LEFT The carnation, as seen here on this antique Eastern European altar cloth, makes an appearance in embroidery the world over.

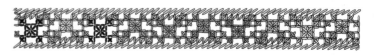

Crewel wall hanging

Crewel work became particularly popular during the seventeenth and eighteenth centuries, and was used for decorating fabrics for curtains, wall hangings and bed hangings. Fine examples of it are to be seen in stately houses in Italy, France, the Low Countries and England.

At that time, the patterns were very large and ornate, and were most commonly based on a "tree-of-life" design. This started with hilly ground at the base, from which huge flowering stems rose up and branched out covered in a wide variety of leaves, blossoms, and berries. Animals, birds and insects often nestled on the ground and also in the branches, filling in most areas of the cloth. Crewel work was predominantly stitched in woollen yarn on linen cloth, but can also be found in silk threads, and nowadays in linen and cotton as well. The colours most commonly seen in this type of work are rich greens, blues and browns, sometimes

peppered with bold reds. Gradually, crewel work evolved and the colours became lighter, and eventually, in the nineteenth century, employed the more repetitive patterns popular at the time.

The design of this piece is a central circle of stylized leaves, berries and flowers which fan out in an even pattern which repeats itself in each quarter. It is stitched onto a background of fine cotton with crewel wool, which is widely available in a multitude of colours and is colourfast and mothproof. However, colours for traditional stranded cotton have also been given.

Transferring this pattern onto cloth would be best done by the "transfer" method described on page 16, as it is quite an intricate design. The pale blue and aqua colours of the wool are cool and calm. You could, of course, change the colours to suit a particular scheme in your house, but do remember that the darker shade should be used for the outline.

RIGHT This symmetrical design is displayed to its best effect as a wall hanging.
ABOVE A flower shape that resembles a carnation forms the central point of the pattern.

ABILITY LEVEL: Intermediate

SIZE OF FINISHED STITCHED AREA:
75 x 75 cm/29½ x 29½in. (Enlarge plan opposite to 400%; reduce above to 80%.)

STRANDED COTTON/EMBROIDERY FLOSS:
3 strands

NEEDLE SIZE: 7

FABRIC:
85 x 85 cm/34 x 34in fine white cotton or linen.

TO MAKE UP
1 Press the cloth so that it is square and even.

2 Roll the cloth carefully around a cardboard cylinder so that it does not crease. Take it to a professional picture framer for mounting and framing.

COLOURS AND STITCHES:

		DMC	Anchor	ACW*
▨	ⓦ	518	779	323
▨	ⓦ	504	847	521

* ACW = Appleton Crewel Wool

Table linen

Pieced tablecloth

This big linen tablecloth is made up of embroidered panels that have been attached to each other by lace borders. There are sixteen pieces arranged around a central square. Each one of these pieces has been decorated with geometric, flower-like motifs and stitched in two soft shades of blue.

The heavy linen cloth has obviously been much laundered over the years, yet despite this it still looks remarkably fresh and crisp. It is certainly worth buying the best quality linen when making tablecloths and napkins, because soiling on linen washes out easily, and the fabric lasts for a long time.

Most of the wide, flat stitching on this cloth is fishbone stitch, which gives slightly more texture than plain satin stitch. Because it makes use of two crossing arms, fishbone is a form of cross stitch. On this cloth, the angle of the crossing stitches in the wide areas of stitching is very relaxed, but in some of the smaller leaves the crossed shape is much more evident.

Because this cloth is made of several panels you could adapt the size to suit your requirements, or alternatively sew only one of the panels to make a placemat.

LEFT A large cloth has been made from squares joined together with cotton lace.
ABOVE Two similar shades of blue add depth and interest to a design.

ABILITY LEVEL: Intermediate

SIZE OF FINISHED CLOTH (WITHOUT LACE BORDER):
160 x 160 cm/63 x 63in. (Enlarge patterns to 122%.)

SIZE OF FINISHED CENTRE SQUARE:
94 x 94 cm/37 x 37in. (Pattern on page 43, when used for the central flowers only, is actual size.)

SIZE OF EACH FINISHED SMALL SQUARE:
29 x 29 cm/11¼ x 11½in

SIZE OF EACH LARGE MOTIF:
24 x 24 cm/9½ x 9½in

STRANDED COTTON/EMBROIDERY FLOSS:
4 strands

NEEDLE SIZE: 5

FABRIC:
Fine white or ivory linen: 16 pieces 32 x 32 cm/13 x 13in square; 1 piece 97 x 97 cm/38 x 38in. Cotton lace for joining: 8 m x 4 cm/8½ yd x 1½in wide. Matching scalloped-edge lace for border; 7m x 8cm/7½yd x 3in wide.

TO MAKE UP
1 Press each piece of cloth so that it is square and even.

2 Take each square and fold 5 mm/¼in over to the wrong side, then another 5 mm/¼in, to make a tiny hem. Mitre corners and pin. Slipstitch in place with matching thread. Hem small squares and big square in the same way.

3 Take the joining lace and cut twelve strips each 32 cm/12½in long. Use each strip to join two small squares together. You want to make two long strips of five squares each (to go down the "sides"), and two smaller strips of three squares each (to go along the "top" and "bottom"). Overlap the lace onto the right side of the squares, leaving about 1 cm/½in protruding at each end. Machine-stitch the edge of the lace to the square. Turn over each raw end and machine-stitch to prevent fraying.

4 Cut two long strips of lace, each 162 cm/64in. Attach the lace to the sides of the central square. Then attach the long strips of squares down each "side" of the central square in the same way. Measure the length of the remaining sides of the central square and cut a further two strips of lace to fit, making sure that you add enough to turn over the raw ends. Attach the shorter strips of squares in the same way.

5 Machine-stitch the edging lace around the edge of the finished cloth.

COLOURS AND STITCHES:

		DMC	Anchor
▨	𝄞 𝄢	3760	131
▢	𝄞 𝄢	519	144

Floral border cloth

This charming tablecloth caught my eye during an outdoor English summer lunch with friends. It had been embroidered by my hostess's mother and represents an excellent example of pretty English embroidery, using a multitude of different stitches.

The embroidery depicts a typical English cottage garden – it is filled with a myriad of flowers,

including hollyhocks, delphiniums, Canterbury bells and daisies – all fresh with very vivid summery colour.

This cloth has been edged in a crisp blue crocheted border. For your floral cloth, you may wish to leave the border plain, however an embroidered tablecloth can look very attractive with an elaborate border. If you are skilled at crochet, there is a wide range of crochet edgings to choose from. Alternatively, if you want a fancy border but can't crochet, you may decide to trim your cloth with purchased cotton lace.

The floral scene on this cloth has been embroidered onto a fine linen damask and – as with some of the finer patterns in this book – should be transferred onto the cloth by the carbon paper method described on page 17.

You should pay special attention to the pattern repeat and the corners. Placement of these should be worked out on the whole cloth before starting to embroider. Indeed, nothing could be more disappointing than a pattern not meeting at the point where it is supposed to.

The cloth as it appears here is a large rectangle, but if that presents too great a project, the same design could be easily reproduced on a smaller, square cloth. This could be achieved by using the pattern as it appears at the shorter ends of the rectangle on each of the four sides.

Remember to use the finest quality linen for the cloth, for ease of laundering.

RIGHT The border on this beautifully stitched cloth depicts a typical English cottage garden.
ABOVE Detail from the floral cloth showing the wide variety of stitches.

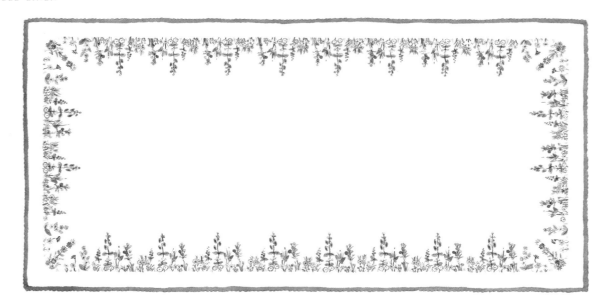

ABILITY LEVEL:
Advanced

SIZE OF FINISHED CLOTH (WITHOUT CROCHET BORDER):
220 x 104 cm/
7ft 2½in x 3ft 5in

LENGTH OF ONE REPEAT PATTERN: 21 cm/8¼in
(enlarge patterns to 115%).

MAXIMUM HEIGHT OF EMBROIDERED PATTERN:
15 cm/6in

MAXIMUM WIDTH OF CROCHETED BORDER:
1.5 cm/⅝in

STRANDED COTTON/EMBROIDERY FLOSS:
4 strands for embroidery; 6 strands for crocheted border

NEEDLE SIZE: 5

FABRIC:
225 x 110 cm/7ft 5in x 3ft 7in good-quality linen damask.

TO MAKE UP

1 Press the cloth so that it is even and square. On each side, measure out 8 cm/3in from the edge of the embroidery, and trim if necessary.

2 Turn 1 cm/⅜in to the wrong side around each edge of the fabric, then another 1.5 cm/⅝in. Press, mitre the corners (see page 21) and pin.

3 Slipstitch the hem invisibly in place, using sewing thread to match.

4 Crochet a scalloped edge around the cloth using the sky-blue cotton.

COLOURS AND STITCHES:

			DMC	Anchor
			B5200	1
			798	131
			809	130
			800	144
			741	314
		○	742	303
			745	300
			893	27
			3716	25
			963	73

			DMC	Anchor
			211	342
			209	109
			208	111
			936	846
			989	242
			988	243
			470	266
			472	278
○			611	898

Peacock cloth

This heavy cloth is exquisitely rich in both colour and design, and epitomizes the symbols and patterns that have evolved in embroidery over the centuries. Indeed, the circles with bursting sun, the figurative peacock and the twisting vines are all derived from historical symbols. And, although the pattern may look like a purely random conglomeration of twisted vines, with birds and decorative wheels scattered here and there, it has in fact been perfectly and logically plotted with repeating areas.

The vivid colours contrast dramatically with the rather austere background linen. Most of the stitching on the cloth is satin stitch, which at first appears to be padded. In fact, it has been worked in thick thread spaced closely together, which gives quite a pleasing, raised shape to the embroidered areas. Another highlight is provided by the yellow areas; they are stitched in shiny  silk, as opposed to the matt surface of the cotton elsewhere.

This is certainly not a project for the novice; it should only be attempted by those experienced with the needle. The transfer of the pattern onto the cloth will be crucial to the overall success, and should be done by the transfer method as described on page 16.

LEFT The rich colours are perfectly displayed on the muted, neutral background.
ABOVE Dense, flat satin stitch gives areas of intense colour.

ABILITY LEVEL: Advanced

SIZE OF FINISHED CLOTH:
103 x 107 cm/40½ x 42in (enlarge pattern overleaf to 198%).

SIZE OF FINISHED STITCHED AREA:
81 x 84 cm/32 x 33in

DIAMETER OF CENTRE CIRCLE:
16.5 cm/6½in

STRANDED COTTON/EMBROIDERY FLOSS:
4 strands

NEEDLE SIZE: 5

FABRIC:
117 x 121 cm/46 x 47½in fine taupe linen or Zweigart 36-count Edinborough 3217 (Linen, Col no 323), or Charles Craft 28/32-count Real Irish Linen (Col "Natural"/ "Tea Dyed").

TO MAKE UP
1 Press the cloth so that it is square and even.

2 Fold 1 cm/⅜in over to the wrong side right around each raw edge, and press. Then fold under another 6 cm/2¼in, to make a wide hem all the way around. Press, mitre the corners (see page 21) and pin.

3 Slipstitch the hem in place with thread that matches the fabric. Alternatively, finish with hem stitch – as on the original.

COLOURS AND STITCHES:

		DMC	Anchor
		973	291
		322	978
		321	9046
		310	403

Tray cloth & napkins

This bright little cloth, embroidered with a pretty floral pattern, would make a perfect wedding or birthday gift. Although it is a relatively simple project to make, I am sure it would always be welcomed by a friend for "the bottom drawer".

The example shown here was probably made in eastern Europe, where red and white have been a continually popular combination – red being a symbol of both life and love. It is decorated with naïve patterns, and uses a wide range of different stitches. Stem stitch has been used for the lines and blanket stitch for the curly fronds. Meanwhile, satin stitch has been used for the leaves, flowers and hearts. These are filled in with a pulled-thread embroidery stitch – four-sided stitch. However, if you prefer not to attempt this, the centres could be left blank. This design would look equally attractive on any other bright primary colour. The cloth is then finished with a narrow hem. It has been folded, quite unusually, onto the right side. It has then been held in place with a decorative zigzag stitch, which seems to add to the generally busy effect of the cloth as a whole.

To make an attractive set, it would be a nice idea to add some embroidered napkins – using the same motif as that of the tray cloth. Indeed, the original cloth, shown here, came with two tiny, matching napkins. Just big enough to catch a few crumbs or for wiping sticky fingers!

RIGHT The combination of red and white is well suited to this bold design.
ABOVE Detail of the floral pattern (actual size).

ABILITY LEVEL: Intermediate

SIZE OF FINISHED CLOTH:
48 x 31 cm/19 x 12½in (enlarge pattern opposite to 112%).

SIZE OF FINISHED NAPKIN:
14 x 14 cm/5½ x 5½in

STRANDED COTTON/ EMBROIDERY FLOSS: 4 strands

NEEDLE SIZE: 5

FABRIC:
One piece 50 x 33 cm/20 x 13in; two pieces 16 x 16 cm/6½ x 6½in fine red cotton.

TO MAKE UP
1 Press the cloth so that it is square and even.

2 Fold 5 mm/¼in over to the right side, right around each raw edge, and press. Then fold another 5 mm/¼in, to make a

tiny hem all the way around. Press and pin.

3 Stitch the hem in place with embroidery cotton, using a zigzag stitch, making every second stitch a backstitch to hold the hem more firmly in place.

COLOURS AND STITCHES:

						DMC	Anchor
☐	✎	▯	⊔⊔	⊞		B5200	1

The matching napkin, showing floral pattern.

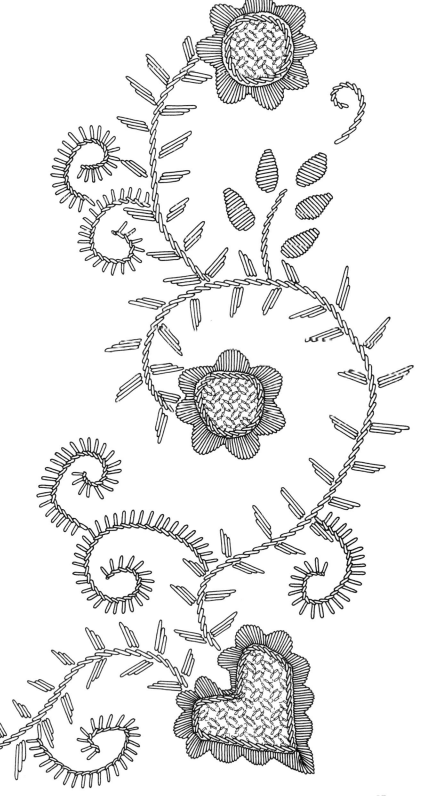

Clover basket liner

This piece, a circular bag-shaped cloth with a pair of finished openings, was found in a country junk shop in France. It was revealed to be a liner for a handled basket; perfect for a bread-basket.

The shape of the liner (see diagram below) must be marked out in order to plot the design. It is probably sensible to keep the fabric whole while embroidering the clover leaves, to avoid the edges fraying. The liner can then be cut out, the seams joined and hem finished, before the decorative border is added.

ABILITY LEVEL: Beginner

SIZE OF FINISHED LINER:
Circumference 103 cm/40½in

**STRANDED
COTTON/EMBROIDERY FLOSS:**
4 strands

NEEDLE SIZE: 5

FABRIC:
53 x 53 cm/21 x 21in loose-woven cream cotton or linen.

60 cm/24in thin bias binding to match.

TO MAKE UP
1 Press the cloth so that it is square and even.

2 Cut two slits, 10 cm/4in long, where indicated (for the basket handles). Bind the slit against fraying: machine-stitch bias binding to the right side of the fabric around the slit, then turn it through to the back and hand-stitch it down.

3 Machine-stitch the four seams, to make the curved shape of the liner. Finish the raw edges to prevent fraying.

4 Fold 5 mm/¼in over to the wrong side right around the raw edge, and press. Then fold another 1 cm/⅜in,

to make a small hem all the way around. Press and pin. Slipstitch the hem in place using sewing thread that matches the fabric.

5 Add the embroidered border.

COLOURS AND STITCHES:

		DMC	Anchor
■	Ⓦ	321	9046

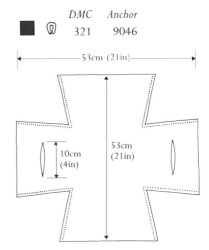

ABOVE A clover leaf is the simple motif for this design. (Reduce pattern to 75%.)
RIGHT Short and long satin stitches cover the hem and make a decorative border.

Bed linen

Lithuanian bedding

This delightful sheet and pillowcase ensemble has been embroidered with cream thread on crisp white, pure cotton. Despite the fact that none of the pieces are antique, they still have a simple and traditional home-made look about them – the embroidery working here to give a cleverly understated effect. And, although they were discovered in a Swedish shop in London, England, they were in fact hand-embroidered in Lithuania.

The set consists of four items: a large sheet, two rectangular pillowcases, and a square pillowcase or cushion cover. The sheet – as detailed in the section overleaf – is big enough to be used on a bed 135 cm (4ft 6in) wide. But it could, of course, be adapted quite easily for any other width or length, depending upon the size of your bed. It is clearly intended to be used as an upper sheet, because the raised texture of the embroidery would certainly not be very comfortable to lie on.

In addition to this, the embroidered border looks extremely pretty folded down and displayed over the top of a blanket. In fact, the smaller top border has been embroidered on the reverse side of the cloth to that of the rest of the embroidery, so that when it is folded over, all the stitching on the entire sheet is displayed on the right side.

The embroidery is made up of a fairly simple flower and garland motif that has been repeated over and over again. It is used as a border on all the pieces and, in different ways, as a central panel on the square pillowcase as well as on the sheet. Each of

the pieces is finished with a plain buttonhole stitch sewn on a scalloped edge.

It is perhaps true to say that completing the entire set would be a time-consuming labour of love. Nevertheless, it would undoubtedly make a priceless heirloom for generations to come.

LEFT   Cream embroidery on white cotton is not an obvious choice, but gives a pretty, understated effect.
ABOVE   Stitch the scallop-shaped edging before trimming the fabric.

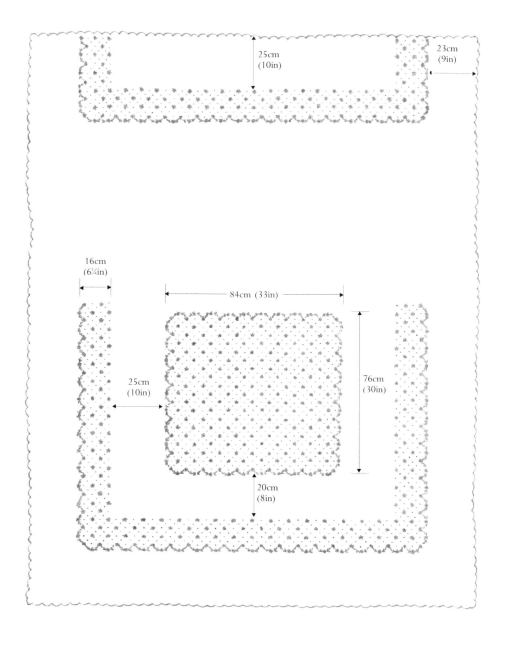

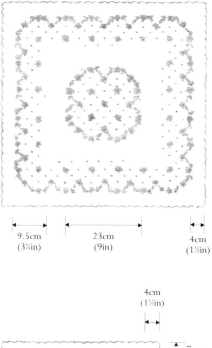

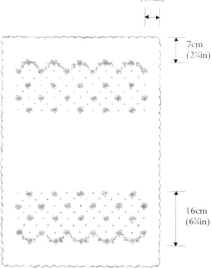

ABILITY LEVEL: Intermediate

SIZE OF FINISHED SHEET:
267 x 212 cm/105 x 83⅓in

WIDTH OF EMBROIDERED BORDER:
16 cm/6¼in

APPROXIMATE WIDTH OF EACH SCALLOP ON EDGING:
2.5 cm/1in

SIZE OF FINISHED RECTANGULAR PILLOWCASE:
70 x 48 cm/27½ x 19in.
(Patterns are actual size.)

SIZE OF FINISHED SQUARE PILLOWCASE:
62 x 62 cm/24½ x 24½in

STRANDED COTTON/EMBROIDERY FLOSS:
3 strands

NEEDLE SIZE: 7

FABRIC:

Cotton sheeting.

SHEET: 2.8 m x (minimum) 220 cm/3yd x 85in wide.

ONE RECTANGULAR PILLOWCASE: two pieces 70 x 48 cm/27⅓ x 19in – embroider front only; strip 48 x 15 cm/19 x 6in for inside flap.

SQUARE PILLOWCASE: two pieces 62 x 62 cm/24½ x 24½in – embroider front only; strip 62 x 15 cm/24½ x 6in for inside flap.

TO MAKE UP

PILLOWCASES:

1 Press the cloth so that it is square and even.

2 Take the narrow strip and make a narrow hem (approximately 1 cm/½in wide) down one of the long sides. Machine-stitch and press. On the other long side, fold over 1 cm/½in to the wrong side and press.

3 Place the embroidered piece right side down on a table. Place the folded edge of the strip down one of its sides (a short side on the rectangular pillowcase), about 1 cm/½in from the edge. Pin them together on the wrong side.

4 Take the plain rectangle or square. Make a small hem (as in step 2 above) down one side (a short side on the rectangular pillowcase).

Machine-stitch and press. On the other three sides, fold over 1 cm/½in to the wrong side and press.

5 Place the plain piece on top of the embroidered piece, wrong sides together, leaving a 1 cm/½in gap all the way around. Pin and machine-stitch the pieces together around all four sides, taking care not to stitch the opening shut.

COLOURS AND STITCHES:

		DMC	Anchor
▨	◫	543	885

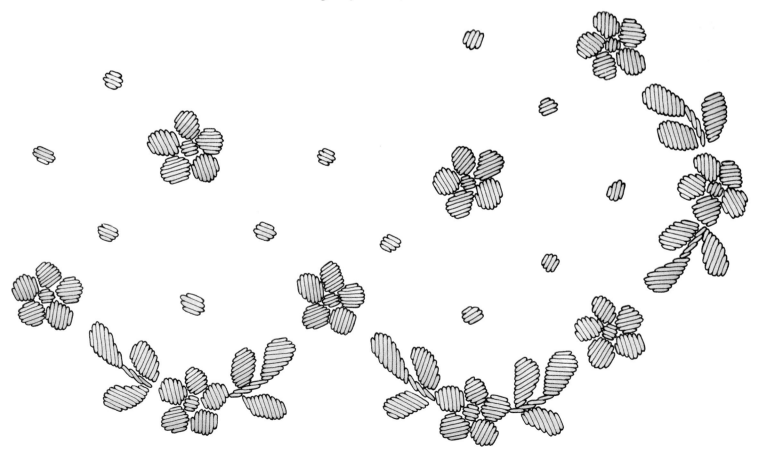

Striped bedspread

This is a somewhat unusual bed covering, probably made in the north of England. It is slightly reminiscent of a Durham quilt or "strippy", commonly made in that part of Britain. And, as it is not at all heavy or warm, it is ideal as a summer coverlet.

There is certainly something naïve and appealing about the simple contrast between the white and the deep red. This effect – which is

accentuated when seen next to white bed linen and pillows – has been achieved by sewing long, embroidered red strips onto a much larger white backing cloth. First, the red fabric has been embroidered with designs of flowers and leaves on a twisting vine, using stem stitch throughout. Then the strips have been attached to the white material using a basic feather stitch.

The large white cloth could be made from cotton sheeting. However, if you would like to use something a little more elaborate, simply join two strips of a narrower fabric together to make a rectangle with a seam down the middle, as the join will be covered by the central red strip.

This cover is a little short by modern standards, so it is a good idea to check and adjust the measurements to suit your own bed, if necessary, before commencing.

RIGHT The popular colours of red and white are combined to good effect with crisp white bed linen and pillows.
ABOVE Stem stitch gives a chunky, solid feel to these simple flower motifs.

ABILITY LEVEL: Intermediate

SIZE OF FINISHED BEDSPREAD:
197 x 215 cm/77½ x 85in. (Enlarge
patterns to 155%.)

WIDTH OF RED STRIPS:
25 cm/10in

**STRANDED COTTON/
EMBROIDERY FLOSS:** 4 strands

NEEDLE SIZE: 5

FABRIC:
Red cotton: 2 m x 90 cm/2¼yd
x 36in wide. Backing material:
2 m x (minimum) 220 cm/
2¼yd x 85in-wide sheeting; or
4 m x 115 cm/4½yd x 45in-
wide cotton or damask.

TO EMBROIDER AND MAKE UP
1 Cut three strips of red cotton
27 cm/11in wide. Embroider two
with pattern A and the third with
pattern B.

2 Cut the white fabric to the
desired width and length, adding
on 8 cm/3¼in (for hems) to both
the length and the width. Join the
white fabric with a central seam, if
necessary. If the fabric has a right
and wrong side, place the wrong
sides together so that the seam is on
the right side of the fabric to be
covered by an embroidered strip.

3 Hem the white fabric all around:
turn over 1 cm/⅜in to the wrong
side, then another 3 cm/1¼in.
Pin and machine stitch.

4 Take the central red strip
(pattern B) and turn over 1 cm/⅜in
to the wrong side on each long side.
Press, and pin the strip down the
centre of the bedspread. Sew the
strip to the backing cloth using
feather stitch.

5 Attach the other two strips in the
same way, using the plan on the
following page.

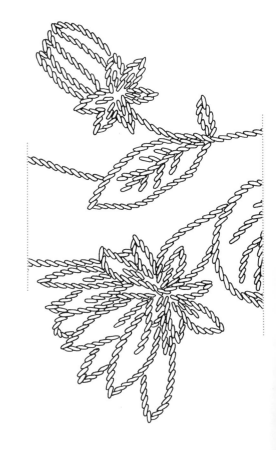

COLOURS AND STITCHES:

	DMC	Anchor
☐ ⊘	B5200	1

40cm (15½in)

30cm (12in)

30cm (12in)

40cm (15½in)

197cm (77½in)

215cm (85in)

Baby's pillowcase

Hand-embroidered gifts are undeniably among the most special presents one can give, and this exquisite, delicate pillow is indeed a treasure to last for generations. The birth of a baby need not be the only excuse to undertake this project, as it would look equally at home in a pretty bedroom, or could even be used as a small cushion cover. And filled with aromatic herbs, it would make a delightful fragrant sleep pillow.

The intricate design of the pillowcase comprises a garland of pastel flowers which has been complemented by an embroidered ribbon of white. All of it is carried out in fine flat satin stitch, using a very fine silky floss, giving the embroidery an attractive sheen which is particularly effective on the ribbon. Special care needs to be taken in the way the stitching runs – it needs to give the illusion of the flat ribbon curling and curving about itself.

The pillowcase illustrated here has been made of the finest quality white cotton lawn. It is edged in a band of the same fabric and pleated gently at the corners to allow it to curve around the right angle. The pillow has been inserted through a buttoned opening in the centre of the back.

A little decorative pillow such as this makes a lasting and special present for the arrival of a child. However, it is important to remember that child-care authorities do not recommend a baby sleeping with a pillow in its cot, due to the danger of suffocation. It is therefore better to keep this pretty item for occasional daytime use.

Because of the delicate nature of the piece, take care to buy the very best quality cotton as well as embroidery silks when choosing the materials for this project – this will also help when it comes to laundering. A factor that is equally crucial to the finished look of this project is the careful finishing of the embroidery – this will prevent the threads from fraying.

RIGHT The crisp white cotton and pretty curving design of this pillowcase would look inviting on any bed.
ABOVE Pay attention to the direction of the stitches to create the illusion of a real ribbon.

ABILITY LEVEL: Intermediate

SIZE OF FINISHED PILLOWCASE:
48.5 x 43 cm/19 x 17in

SIZE OF EMBROIDERED AREA:
30 x 27.5 cm/12 x 11in (patterns are actual size).

**STRANDED COTTON/
EMBROIDERY FLOSS:** 1 strand

NEEDLE SIZE: 9

FABRIC:
Four pieces of fine white cotton lawn: one 39.5 x 33 cm/ 15½ x 13in for embroidered front; a strip 14 x 175 cm/ 5½ x 69in for edging; two 20.5 x 39 cm/8 x 15 ½in, for back with centre opening.
Three 1 cm/⅜in white buttons.

TO MAKE UP
1 Press the embroidered piece so that it is square and even.

2 Take the two pieces for the back of the pillowcase. On each piece, on one of the sides measuring 39 cm/15¼in, turn over to the wrong side 5 mm/¼in, then another 2 cm/¾in to make a hem. Pin, press and machine-stitch.

3 Along one of the hems, measure in 10 cm/4in from each raw edge. Make a buttonhole, parallel to the hem, at each point. Make another buttonhole in the centre of the hem,

between these two buttonholes. Lap that hem over the other and sew on the buttons in the appropriate places.

4 Take the long strip of material, fold it in half lengthways and press. Open it up again and pin the two narrow ends together, allowing 1 cm/⅜in seam. Machine-stitch, and press the seam open. Fold the strip over again.

5 Start pinning the edging to the right side of the embroidered material. Align the raw edges, with the fold pointing into the centre of the rectangle, and allow a 1 cm/⅜in seam all the way around. At each corner, pleat the edging with four 1 cm/⅜in tucks so that it can reach around the corner. Make sure that the seam is hidden in one of the corner pleats.

If necessary, carefully pin the edging down near its fold in order to keep it out of the way of the seam.

6 Machine-stitch the edging to the embroidered material only, 8 mm/¼in in from the raw edges.

7 Place the buttoned back pieces over the embroidered material, right sides together, and pin around all four sides, allowing a 1 cm/⅜in seam. Machine-stitch just in toward the centre from the previous line of stitching, so that it will not show when the pillow is turned right side out.

8 Undo the buttons, turn the cover right side out, unpin the edging and insert the pillow.

COLOURS AND STITCHES:

		DMC	Anchor
■	◫	3716	25
■	◫	800	130
■	◫	745	300
■	◫	3348	240
□	◫	B5200	1

Cot coverlet

This sweet cot coverlet, with embroidered sprigs and bouquets of country flowers scattered across it, could easily become a family heirloom. Wouldn't it be a good idea to rekindle the old tradition of a family cot cover and embroider it for the arrival of a new family member? It could be passed on to subsequent generations and would undoubtedly be valued for many years to come.

The age-old tradition of embroidering pieces for births and marriages seems – sadly – to have dwindled somewhat in recent years, but it certainly seems to be worthy of another revival.

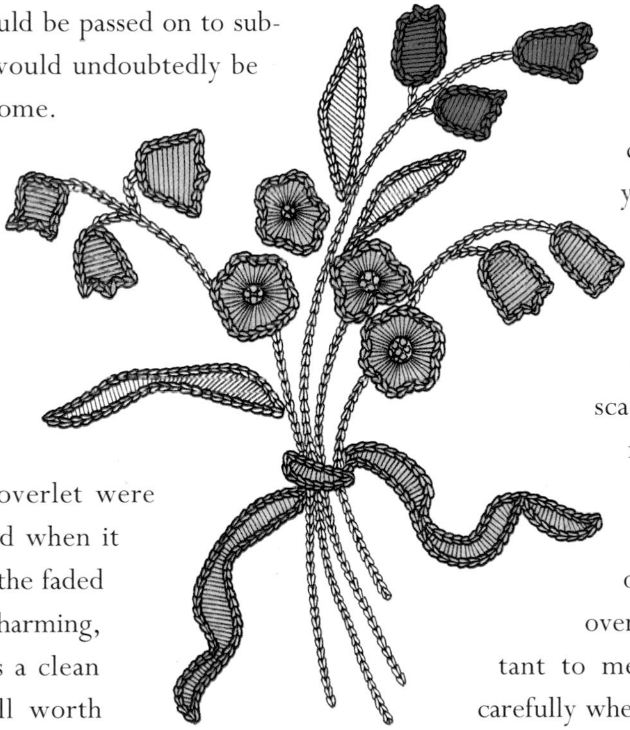

The colours on this coverlet were probably much more vivid when it was first made. However, the faded shades now appear quite charming, and the fabric still retains a clean and fresh look. It is well worth investing in high quality linen or cotton – it will ultimately be more likely to survive the constant laundering required by almost anything used around babies. In this particular case, the fabric needs to be very dense and fine, as the stitches are reasonably small. The embroidery has been undertaken in a dense satin stitch, and then outlined in very fine chain stitch.

Although the pattern has been very carefully thought out and planned on the coverlet shown here, you could certainly alter it and make up your own, more random pattern if you wish. Your own personal pattern could consist of embroidered sprigs and bunches all scattered unevenly over the material. If, however, you would prefer to adhere to the specified arrangement of the pattern (as described overleaf) it is particularly important to measure out your areas very carefully when transferring it.

The pattern here would also be applicable for a duvet cover for a little girl's room. Simply repeat the overall design, and make it up to the size of the duvet required.

LEFT Embroider these delightful flowers on fine linen or cotton – it feels very crisp to the touch and is easy to keep clean.
ABOVE Detail of the coverlet's floral pattern. You may wish to adapt this pattern, perhaps making it more random.

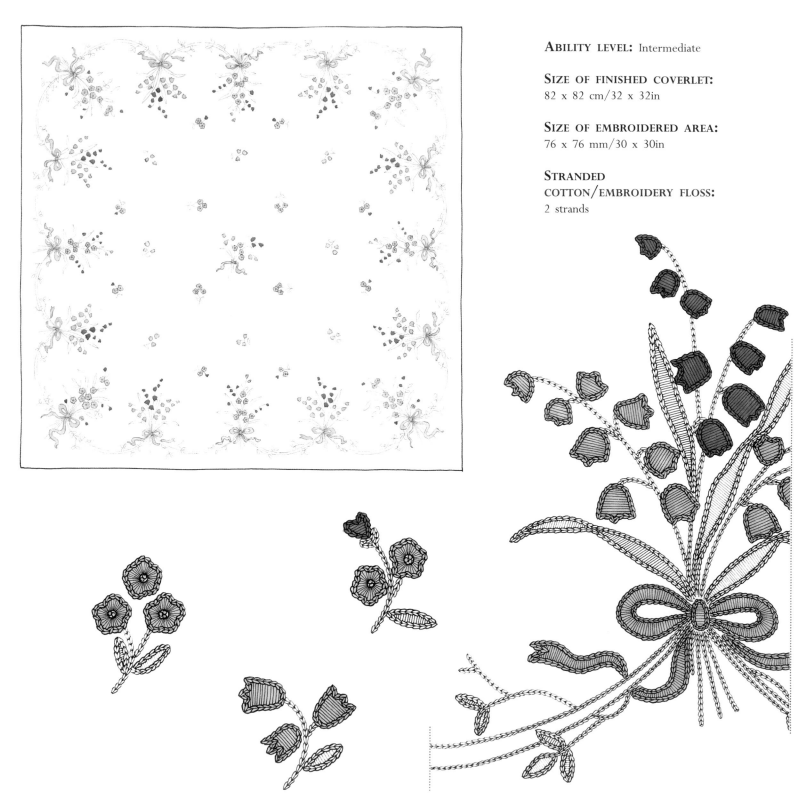

ABILITY LEVEL: Intermediate

SIZE OF FINISHED COVERLET:
82 x 82 cm/32 x 32in

SIZE OF EMBROIDERED AREA:
76 x 76 mm/30 x 30in

**STRANDED
COTTON/EMBROIDERY FLOSS:**
2 strands

NEEDLE SIZE: 8

FABRIC: 88 x 88 cm/35 x 35in heavy white cotton or linen. (Patterns here are actual size.)

TO MAKE UP

1 Press the cloth so that it is square and even.

2 Place the cloth wrong side up. On each of the side edges, turn over 1 cm/⅜in, then another 2 cm/¾in to make a hem. Press, mitre the corners carefully (see page 21) and pin.

3 Slipstitch in place using matching thread.

COLOURS AND STITCHES:

			DMC	Anchor
	‖	∩	676	891
	‖	∩	3328	42
	‖	∩	776	26
	‖	∩	3752	120
	‖	∩	B5200	1

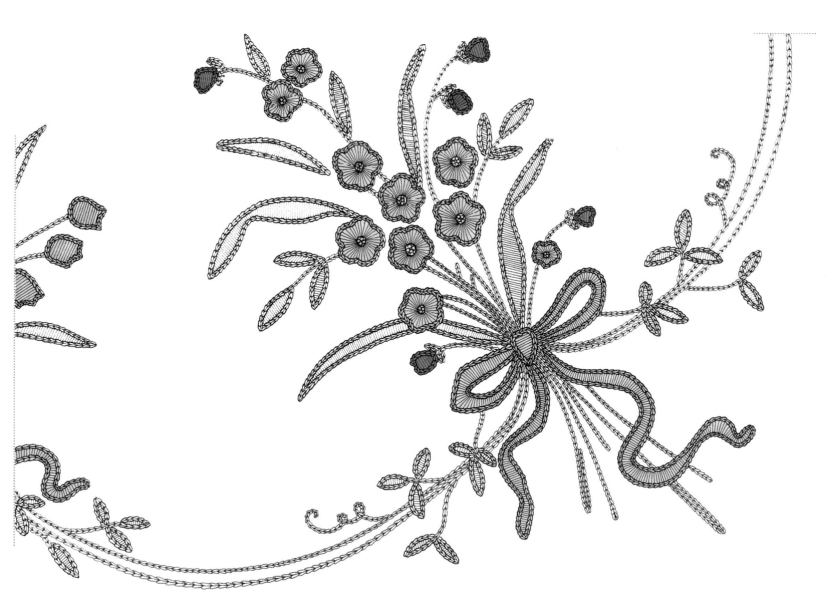

Irish nightdress case

Montmellick is the name of a village near Waterford in Ireland. At the time of the Industrial Revolution in the second half of the nineteenth century, work was hard to find. This prompted a local resident, Mrs Johanna Carter, to set up a school for needlewomen, making household goods to sell.

Many different sorts of items were embroidered, but mainly bed spreads, tablecloths, cushions, nightdress cases and cot sheets. All the items were embroidered in the same manner and style, which subsequently became known as Montmellick embroidery. The central feature of this embroidery is the somewhat coarse, durable stitchery, where there are very few or no open spaces. The same heavy cotton thread was always used, usually on a lustrous white cotton, and pieces can be easily recognized by the trademark of a heavy looped and distinctive fringe.

The nightdress case shown here is a good example of Montmellick work. It has a wide variety of stitches, which therefore makes it an interesting work to copy today. The motifs on the piece are largely of the floral/leaf kind – as can be seen in detail overleaf.

The distinctive fringe has actually been knitted separately and then sewn to the edges of the embroidered piece. You could, of course, improvise and replace it by heavy white cotton lace – this would create an equally attractive effect. Alternatively, you could extend the measurements given below by about 4cm/1½in all around, to make a fringe from the material itself. To avoid further fraying after the fringe has been completed, it could be held in place by the blanket stitch border that edges the original piece.

LEFT This nightdress case from Montmellick in Ireland is a typical example of the embroidery from that village. It has a wide variety of stitches and a looped fringe.

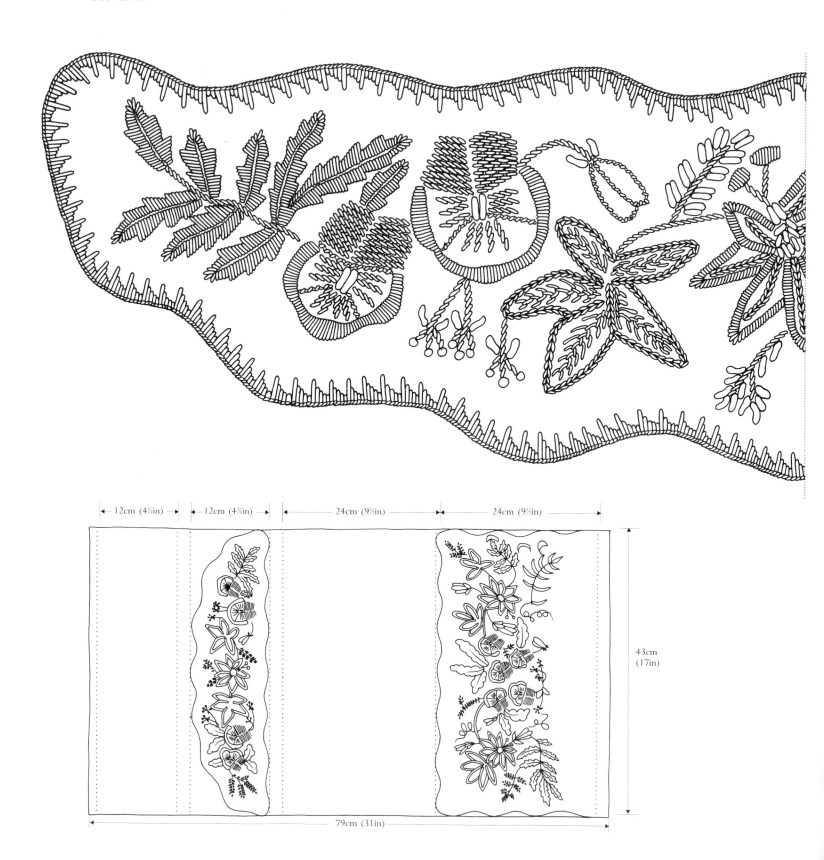

ABILITY LEVEL: Advanced

SIZE OF FINISHED CASE (EXCLUDING FRINGE):
41 x 27 cm/16 x 10½in. (Enlarge all patterns to 110%.)

STRANDED COTTON/ EMBROIDERY FLOSS: 3 strands

NEEDLE SIZE: 7

FABRIC:
43 x 79 cm/17 x 31in white cotton.

TO MAKE UP

1 Embroider the piece according to the plan. Press.

2 Hem the edge that will make the top part of the pocket by turning over 1 cm/⅜in to the wrong side, followed by another 1 cm/⅜in. Pin and slipstitch. Press. On the other short edge, turn over 1 cm/⅜in to the wrong side. Press.

3 Fold over the edge that has been hemmed, right sides together, to make a pocket 24 cm/9½in deep. Press, pin and machine-stitch down each side. (The machine-stitching can be straight, or curved as on the original.)

4 Fold over the other edge, right sides together, to make a pocket 12 cm/4¾in deep. Press, pin, and mark the curved seam line according to the embroidery. Machine-stitch, and trim the seams back to 1 cm/⅜in.

5 Turn the bag right side out, and pin the lower edge of the upper flap in place. Slipstitch.

6 Add cotton lace right around each side of the bag, if desired.

COLOURS AND STITCHES:

		DMC	Anchor
☐	𝄐 𝄐 𝄐 𝄐	B5200	1
	𝄐 𝄐 𝄐 𝄐		
	𝄐		

Monograms

Monograms

The word monogram comes from the ancient Greek words meaning single and line (or single letter), and was at one time also used to signify a picture drawn in lines without shading or colour. A monogram later came to be known as a motif composed of two or more letters intertwined together, the letters usually being the initials of a person's name. Monograms, also sometimes known as ciphers, were first used on letters or seals, and many early Greek and Roman coins show the monograms of rulers or towns. The most famous is known as the sacred monogram and is formed by joining first two letters of the Greek word for Christ. It sometimes appears with the characters for alpha and omega on either side.

During the Middle Ages a large number of monograms were created, by religious institutions, craftsmen and businessmen. Monograms or ciphers were employed by the first printers, and are now helpful in working out the origins of early printed

books. Similar motifs were also used by engravers and manufacturers of pottery. Medieval merchants often used their own specific symbols to identify their goods; these consisted of their initials and other marks such as a Christian cross.

Monograms have been embroidered on household linens and clothing for hundreds of years. These were primarily for identification purposes – probably for when the items were taken out of the house for laundering, or possibly even to guard against theft. However, many of them became wonderfully decorative embellishments and ornamentation in their own right, and are now associated with high status and wealth.

The letters overleaf show you how you can embroider your own monograms. They are usually worked in a dense satin stitch to create a solid band of colour. This delightful art form will impart a sense of expensive luxury to any item to which they are added.

RIGHT Many styles of typography can be used for monogrammed initials, including the Gothic and medieval types seen here. ABOVE A stylized crown conveys a sense of rank and wealth when combined with interwoven initials.

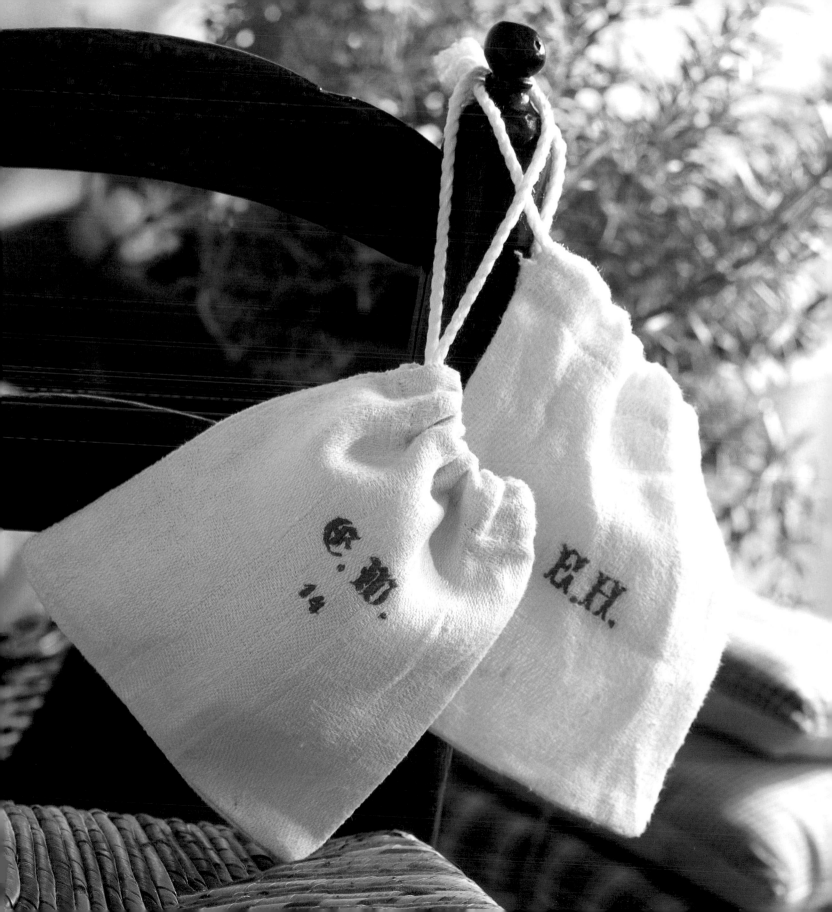

A B C D E F G

a b c d e f g h i j k

N O P P 2 R S

u v w x y z &

H I J K L M

l m n o p q r s t

T U V W X Y Z

Use these letters to embroider your own mongrams. To create a solid band of colour, work the letters in dense satin stitch, or stem and back stitch, as has been done here.

Accessories

Window pelmet

Although these heavily embroidered pieces were found in the south of France, there is a definite Eastern European feel suggested both by the colour and pattern. It had been used as a runner cloth in a farmhouse, to protect the wood on an antique carved oak trunk, but it now makes a delightfully bold curtain pelmet or valance and would give any bedroom a country-cottage look.

Here, the pelmet has been clipped to a wrought-iron curtain pole, but it could just as easily be attached to a standard pelmet board, using Velcro or touch-and-close fastening hand-stitched to the back. Either method allows easy removal for washing or dry cleaning. If the measurements specified overleaf do not fit your window you can, of course, adjust the embroidery to fit in various ways, such as making the motifs smaller or increasing the amount of space between them.

The embroidery thread is thick and is stitched closely together, which serves to give an attractive, raised pattern. Some of the pattern has been sewn in an off-white that is hardly different from the colour of the cloth, and therefore adds to the texture rather than contributing any discernable colour. The scalloped edges are finished in blanket stitch. You may find it easiest to embroider the scallop shapes before trimming the material to the correct shape – taking care, of course, not to snip any of the stitches. If you are unsure how to proceed, experiment first on a scrap of spare fabric.

As with some of the more intricate patterns in this book, the plotting of the pattern is particularly crucial, and the best method is probably the carbon method (see page 17). Do remember to work the embroidery from the centre outward.

LEFT Create a European, cottagey feel in a bedroom by combining this bold pelmet with matching plain curtains and tie-backs.

ABILITY LEVEL: Intermediate

SIZE OF FINISHED PELMET:
142 x 39 cm/56 x 15⅓in. (Enlarge above pattern to 350%.)

STRANDED COTTON/ EMBROIDERY FLOSS: 4 strands

NEEDLE SIZE: 5

FABRIC:
148 x 45 cm/58 x 18in heavy white cotton or linen, or Zweigart 25-count Dublin 3604 (Linen, Col no 222), or Charles Craft 28-count Real Irish Linen (Col "Cream").

TO EMBROIDER AND MAKE UP
1 Work the central sections of embroidery before the red scallops and off-white circles of the edging.

2 Press the cloth so that it is square and even. Measure out and mark the scallops around the edge.

3 Stitch the buttonhole scallops and then carefully trim the material around them.

4 Add the off-white circles inside each of the scallops.

5 Carefully hand-stitch the pelmet fastening – loops or Velcro – to the back of the embroidery.

COLOURS AND STITCHES:

		DMC	Anchor
		347	799
		ECRU	2

Curtain tie-backs

Tie-backs perform a dual function. On a purely practical level, they hold back curtains from windows to let in the maximum amount of light; they can also, of course, look very attractive. Indeed, the plainest curtains can be transformed

when caught back with attractive tie-backs – they can often add both decorative detail and a pleasing shape to the window dressing. Embroidery lends itself beautifully to tie-backs of all sorts, and there are two here to inspire the busy embroiderer. The plainer, white tie-backs are made from a

wide band of fine white cotton. They have been embellished with a flowery, swirling pattern in chunky white chain stitch, and interlined to give a slightly padded look. The edges have been piped in a fresh red and white gingham, cut on the cross, with little narrow ties.

In contrast, the other pair of tie-backs are highly colourful. The vibrant floral design has been satin-stitched in coton perlé – a shiny, silky cotton that does not have divisible strands like regular embroidery thread or floss.

These curved floral tie-backs (on page 100) are shaped specially for holding back curtains, and are edged with a very pretty blue herringbone-stitched border. The narrow ribbon ties have been made from two strips of bias binding, which have been machined together with a zigzag stitch. However, you could just as easily substitute a ribbon in a matching colour.

While sample measurements are given for these projects overleaf, it would obviously be a good idea to check – before you commence – that the tie-backs are suitable for your particular curtains. Make a paper template according to the dimensions given here, or use a tape measure to check the length required.

RIGHT   Padding has been added here to give a reassuringly solid feel, and to complement the tie-back's prosaic shape and simple embroidery.

ABOVE   Cut on a curve to make a pleasing shape, this brightly coloured tie-back would look best with plain curtains.

WHITE TIE-BACKS

ABILITY LEVEL: Intermediate

SIZE OF FINISHED TIE-BACK:
64 x 18 cm/25 x 7in (enlarge above pattern to 150%)

STRANDED COTTON/EMBROIDERY FLOSS:
6 strands

NEEDLE SIZE: 5

FABRIC:
Four pieces 67 x 21 cm/25½ x 8¼in medium/heavy white cotton.
Two pieces 67 x 21 cm/25¼ x 8¼in thin wadding or interlining.
One piece 1 m/1yd fine-checked cotton gingham.
3.5 m/4yd piping cord.

TO MAKE UP

1 Stitch the pattern on two pieces of the cotton, leaving a border of at least 1.5 cm/⅝in around the edges. Press.

2 Take one of the other pieces of cotton, and the wadding. Pin the wadding to the wrong side, and machine-stitch the wadding and cotton together around the edges, 1 cm/⅜in from the raw edge.

3 Now make the piping. Cut 4 cm/1½in-wide diagonal strips from the red gingham, and join them with diagonal seams to make a length to go around the outside of the tie-back, plus about 3 cm/1¼in (about 170 cm/67in for each tie-back).

Press the seams open. Fold in 1.5 cm/⅝in at one end of the strip and press. Lay the cord in the centre of the wrong side with the end tucked under the turn-back. Fold the strip over the cord, matching the raw edges. Machine-stitch close to the cord with a zipper foot.

4 Placing right sides and raw edges (of plain pieces) together, pin piped strip to the white cotton 1.5 cm/⅝in in from edge. Machine-stitch about 12 mm/½in in from edge.

5 Make the gingham ties for each end, from material cut on the straight grain. Those on the sample measure 22 x 2 cm/8½ x ¼in when finished. Pin them at either end of the tie-back, with the raw end at the seam line and other end pointing into the centre of the tie-back.

6 Place the two pieces, right sides together, on top of each other and pin. Starting on one of the long sides, machine-stitch (with a zipper foot) almost all the way around,

1.5 cm/⅝in in from the raw edge, and leaving a gap in the stitching of about 10 cm/4in. Make sure that the ties are included at each end, and reinforce the stitching there, if necessary. Trim the raw edges to 1 cm/⅜in.

7 Turn the tie-back right side out, and slipstitch the opening closed.

COLOURS AND STITCHES:

	DMC	Anchor
☐ ⓠ	B5200	1

CURVED FLORAL TIE-BACKS

ABILITY LEVEL: Intermediate

WIDTH OF FINISHED TIE-BACK:
7 cm/2¾in

PEARL COTTON/COTON PERLÉ
Do not divide strands

NEEDLE SIZE: 3

FABRIC:
Two pieces 43 x 23 cm/17 x 9in
cream cotton or linen.
2.4 m/2yd bias binding or 1 cm/
⅜in-wide ribbon

TO EMBROIDER AND MAKE UP
1 Mark out the shape of the tie-back
on the material (pattern below is
actual size), plus a border all around
of 1.5cm/⅝in, but do not cut them.

Embroider the floral pattern on the cotton, and press. Cut the material to the correct shape, including the extra border as above.

2 Place the material wrong side up. Around each side, fold over 5 mm/¼in, then another 1cm/⅜in to make a hem. Pin, press and slipstitch in place.

3 Embroider the herringbone pattern around the border, and attach the ties.

COLOURS AND STITCHES:

		DMC	Anchor
		796	133
		368	242
		816	20
		891	28
		700	229
		743	290
		780	370

Tree of life hand towel

This little hand towel is an excellent project for the embroidery novice to tackle. It is made of unbleached linen and has been embroidered with a plain off-white cotton. Linen is particularly suitable for towels as it absorbs water more easily than any other fibre.

Hand embroidered in Lithuania, the towel carries a simple and charming "tree of life" pattern. It is one of the most common, and effective, motifs in embroidery the world over, and represents birth, life, death and rebirth in the branching of leaves and vines. Such trees are often topped with stylized birds that symbolize the spiritual world, as can be seen in this partic- ular design. There is a lovely free-form feel about this pattern which gives it a naive and some- what primitive look, that makes it very appealing. The motifs are used very effectively, almost appearing three-dimensional.

The embroidery stitches needed here, namely satin, stem, buttonhole and herringbone,

are quite straightforward, and so this is certainly a good beginner's project, and is par- ticularly useful for practising needle skills.

Although the measurements have been given on the following pages, it is certainly worth consider- ing precisely where on the hand towel you intend to place the embroidery.

This does not present a problem if the towel is simply ironed and folded. However, if it is to be hung on a rail or loop, the pattern will be either not visible, or upside-down. If that is likely to be the case, the motif could easily be moved around by 180 degrees so that the top is close to the edge. Alternatively, it could be placed in two corners of the towel. If you want to use the pattern for something other than a towel, it would be particularly effective stitched onto the centre of a cushion.

Whatever your preference, do make sure that the stitches are started and finished off firmly so that the wear and tear caused by hands, and frequent laundering, does not unravel them.

RIGHT Natural colours and materials show off this traditional European design to perfection.
ABOVE AND OVERLEAF The design of the hand towel consists of a "tree of life", with stylized birds.

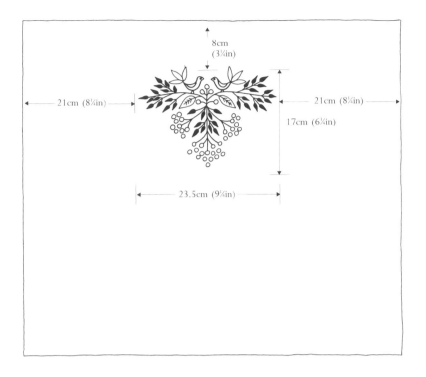

8cm
(3¼in)

21cm (8¼in)

21cm (8¼in)

17cm (6¾in)

23.5cm (9¼in)

ABILITY LEVEL: Beginner

SIZE OF FINISHED TOWEL:
65 x 57 cm/25½ x 22½in

SIZE OF EMBROIDERED AREA:
23.5 x 17 cm/9¼ x 6¾in. (Enlarge
pattern opposite to 118%.)

**STRANDED COTTON/
EMBROIDERY FLOSS:** 3 strands

NEEDLE SIZE: 7

FABRIC:
74 x 66 cm/29 x 26in natural-
coloured linen, or Zweigart 25-
count Dublin 3604 (Linen, Col no
53), or Charles Craft 28-count
Real Irish Linen (Col "Natural"
or "Tea Dyed").

TO MAKE UP

1 Press the cloth so that it is square and even.

2 Place the cloth wrong side up. On each of the side edges, turn over 1 cm/⅜in, then another 3.5 cm/

1¼in to make a hem. Press, mitre the corners carefully (see page 21) and pin.

3 Machine-stitch in place using matching thread.

COLOURS AND STITCHES:

		DMC	Anchor
▨ ⬭〰〰🔧 ⧓⧓ ⧈	ECRU		2

105

Sponge bag

This pretty sponge bag is evocative of 1940s embroidery: very colourful with lots of flowers, and occasionally some stylized people or animals. Here, the little clusters of flowers – in lazy-daisy stitch – are grouped along a twisting green vine, forming a symmetrical pattern. At the centre of the design is the ornately dressed flower girl, who is seen presiding over her garden of colour.

The sponge bag itself is made out of crisp mint-green striped cotton. It has a zip along one long side which has been hidden by the

lace-edged embroidered flaps that fall on either side. Each white cotton flap has been edged by sewn-on, white crochet lace. If you prefer, you could make the bag and flaps from the same material.

An obvious prerequisite for a sponge bag is for it to be washable. The lining in this particular bag is plastic, making it much more practical than it otherwise looks. You can always buy a ready-made bag and attach the embroidered flaps – which would make an ordinary bag into a treasured gift. Alternatively, you could adapt this design to a little cushion or a nightdress holder.

LEFT AND ABOVE   Three simple stitches are all that is necessary to carry out this charming, symmetrical floral design.

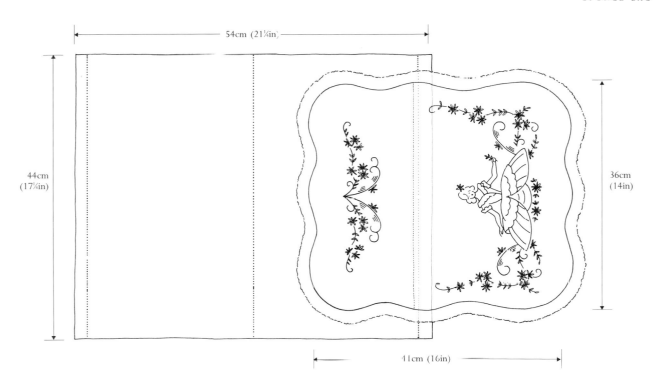

54cm (21¼in)

44cm (17¼in)

36cm (14in)

41cm (16in)

ABILITY LEVEL: Beginner

SIZE OF FINISHED BAG:
41 x 26 cm/16 x 10¼in

SIZE OF EMBROIDERED FLAPS:
41 x 36 cm/16 x 14in (enlarge
patterns to 140%).

**STRANDED COTTON/
EMBROIDERY FLOSS:** 3 strands

NEEDLE SIZE: 7

FABRIC:
41 x 36 cm/16 x 14in white
cotton. 54 x 44 cm/21¼ x
17¼in fine-striped cotton.
Same size of flexible plastic
for lining, if desired.
36 cm/14in white zip.
2 m x 2 cm/2yd x ¾in-wide
heavy white cotton lace.

TO MAKE UP

1 Embroider the white cotton for
the flaps. Cut the curved edges (no
seam allowance is necessary) and pin
on the lace edging, lapping it over
the raw edges by about 3 mm/⅛in.
Machine-stitch with a fine zigzag.

2 Make the sponge bag from the
striped material. On each of the two
short edges, fold over 1.5 cm/⅝in,
wrong sides together. Press. Pin
the closed zip to the folded edges,
so that the other raw edges match
evenly. Machine-stitch, trim the
short raw edges back to the zip,
then zigzag stitch.

3 Open the zip, and turn the bag
inside out. Pin a 1.5 cm/⅝in seam
down each side. Machine-stitch
and finish the raw edges. Turn
the bag right side out.

(Make the plastic lining, if desired,
and insert into the bag, attaching it
to the material around the zip.)

4 Pin the embroidered flaps to the
bag, down one side of the zip.
Make sure that the bigger flap is the
one that goes over the zip to hide
it. Machine-stitch or backstitch the
flap along the side of the zip,
allowing the zip enough room
to function.

COLOURS AND STITCHES:

			DMC	Anchor
	🧵 👐		603	27
	👐		208	111
	🧵 👐		666	46
	👐		996	433
	👐 👐		743	302
	🧵 ○		826	147
	🧵		700	228
	🧵 ○		310	403

Christmas runner

The holly pattern and colour of this cloth makes it very suitable as a Christmas decoration.

The pattern looks involved, but is actually a simple leaf and berry motif, repeated over and over again, first one way and then flipped in a mirror image of itself for a continuous but symmetrical effect. The stitching is plain: stem stitch for the outlines and a raised satin stitch for the berries. The three-dimensional look of the berries is achieved by sewing one layer of satin stitch over the required area, and covering it with other layers until the desired roundness is reached.

The scalloped border alternates curves of different sizes for a slightly more complex look than is usual. It has also been stitched in embroidery thread by hand, but if you are short of time and have a good-quality sewing machine, it could possibly be finished on the machine. You may wish to simplify the scallops, and stitch them before carefully trimming the cloth around them.

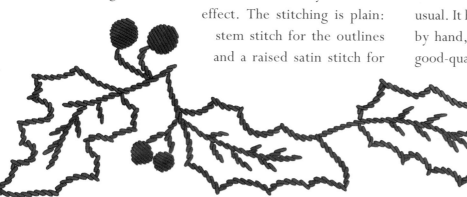

ABILITY LEVEL: Intermediate

SIZE OF FINISHED CLOTH:
94 x 23 cm/37 x 9in

STRANDED COTTON/EMBROIDERY FLOSS:
4 strands

NEEDLE SIZE: 5

FABRIC:
98 x 32 cm/38½ x 12½in cream

cotton or linen, or Zweigart 28-count Jubilee 3232 (Cotton, Col no 225), or Charles Craft 28-count Real Irish Linen (Col "Cream").

TO MAKE UP
1 Complete the holly embroidery, but do not stitch the scalloped edge.

2 Press the cloth so that it is square and even.

3 Place the cloth wrong side up.

On the top edge, turn over 1 cm/⅜in, then another 3 cm/1¼in to make a hem. Press and machine-stitch in place using matching thread.

4 Cut the material into a scalloped shape and stitch the buttonholed edge around the other three sides.

COLOURS AND STITCHES:

		DMC	Anchor
■	∅ ◑	321	47

RIGHT Two lines of the same embroidery and a scalloped edge (in buttonhole stitch) make up this festive cloth.

ABOVE The holly/berry motif is used repeatedly; first one way and then in its mirror image. Reduce the pattern to 95%.

Napkin holder

This small, envelope-like bag was originally used as a folder for storing a table napkin. Today, although this tradition has largely been discontinued, the bag would make a sweet and thoughtful present, and could be used for all sorts of purposes: storing handkerchieves with lavender, or holding oddments while travelling. This is also a good project for a beginner: it is easy and quick to make.

ABILITY LEVEL: Beginner

SIZE OF FINISHED HOLDER:
28 x 13 cm/11 x 5in

SIZE OF CENTRAL MOTIF:
107 x 36 mm/4¼ x 1⅜in

STRANDED COTTON/EMBROIDERY FLOSS:
6 strands

NEEDLE SIZE: 5

FABRIC:
34 x 32 cm/13½ x 12⅓in fine white cotton or linen.
Two matching buttons, 11 mm/½in

TO MAKE UP AND EMBROIDER
1 Press the cloth so that it is square and even.

2 Place the cloth wrong side up. On one of the sides measuring 30 cm/12in turn over 1cm/⅜in, then another 1 cm/⅜in to make a small hem. Press, pin and machine-stitch with matching thread.

3 Fold the material over, right sides together, to make a pocket 12 cm/4¾in deep. The hem should form the edge of the pocket. Pin a seam 2 cm/¾in in from the raw edges and machine-stitch.

4 Trim the corners of the flap diagonally, then fold the edges of the flap over (as in step 2) to make a 1 cm/⅜in hem. Slipstitch the hem in matching thread, then trim the seams so that they are approximately 1 cm/⅜in wide.

5 The piece is now ready for embroidering. Also using embroidery thread, sew on loops and attach the buttons.

COLOURS AND STITCHES:

		DMC	Anchor
■ ⌀ ▯ ○		321	288

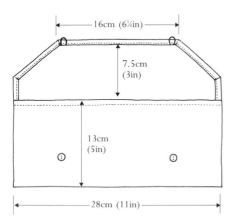

ABOVE You can use this simple floral motif on other items such as handkerchieves or napkins. (Floral pattern above is actual size.)

LEFT This rectangular bag is useful for many purposes and would make a delightful gift.

Beginners' cushion

Here is a perfect project for the beginner. This unusual little cushion has been made out of a traditional linen tea towel. It was woven with red lines that make regular squares on a white background, making an ideal grid to keep the design on the straight and narrow. The simplistic pattern is effective and charming, using cross stitches of various sizes superimposed onto each other, with running stitches anchoring the long ends, to make a star-like motif. The cushion has been personalized with the initials, E. K. W., cross-stitched not quite in the centre, giving it a quirky appearance. A border of feather stitch has been sewn right around the edge.

ABILITY LEVEL: Beginner

SIZE OF FINISHED CUSHION:
26 x 21 cm/10¼ x 8¼in

STRANDED COTTON/EMBROIDERY FLOSS:
4 strands

NEEDLE SIZE: 5

FABRIC:
Two pieces 29 x 24 cm/11½ x 9½in. Cushion stuffing.

STAR MOTIF
1 Stitch a large cross stitch. It should run parallel to the woven grid square.

2 Stitch another large cross stitch over the first, running along the diagonals of the square.

3 Stitch a small cross stitch in the centre, over the large cross stitches, to anchor them.

4 Make small running stitches over each end of the large cross stitches.

TO MAKE UP
1 Press the embroidered piece so that it is square and even.

2 Place the two pieces right sides together and pin, allowing a 1.5 cm/⅝in seam all around. Machine-stitch, leaving a gap of about 7.5

cm/3in in one side, through which to insert the stuffing.

3 Turn the cushion right side out, stuff it, and then slipstitch the opening closed.

COLOURS AND STITCHES:

			DMC	Anchor
■	✎	✄	304	19

RIGHT AND ABOVE The woven squares on this material provide a handy grid for plotting the star-like pattern of combined cross stitches. Reduce the pattern above by 50%.

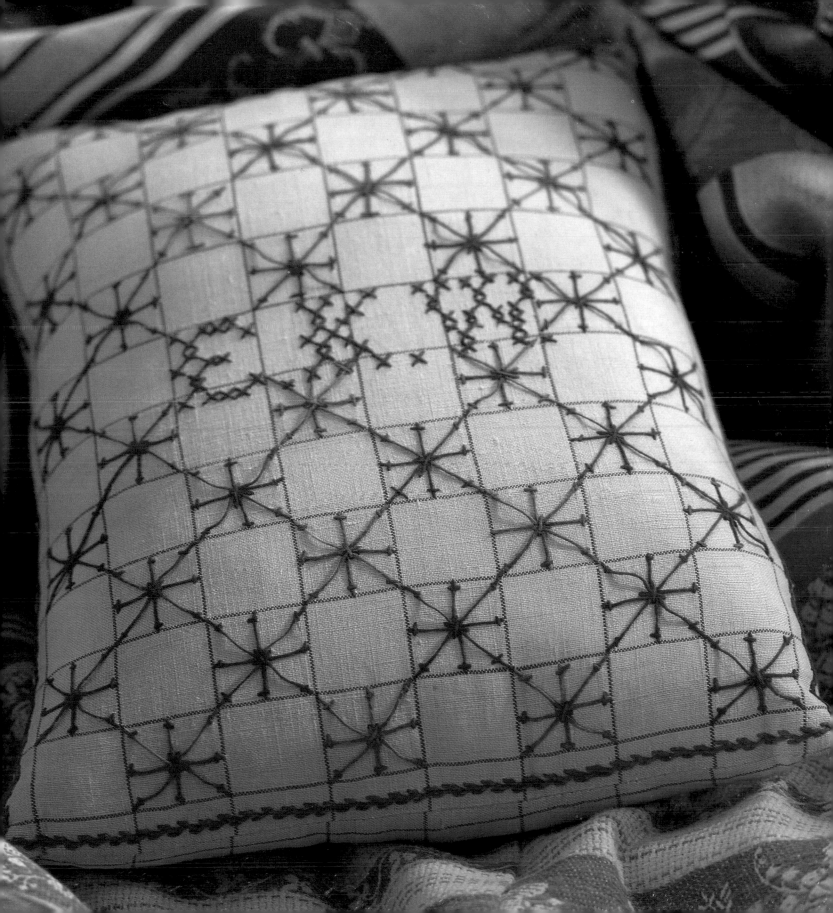

Floral pincushion

This rectangular pincushion has been made from an antique piece of embroidery too small for anything else yet too special to waste. The bunches of flowers alternate in colours, giving the piece a rustic look. Although the exact colours have been specified below, it would be perfectly acceptable to use up thread left over from other projects.

The original stitching is extremely fine, using tiny chain stitches for the leaves and most of the flowers, with a sort of zigzagged back stitch for the brown stems and a fine back stitch for the flower on the left outlined in green. If the stitches are too fine for working comfortably, try using a large magnifying glass or enlarging the motif. The secret of a good pincushion is stuffing it very full and evenly. This makes it easier for the pins to stay in place. Using oddments of wool for stuffing will discourage pins and needles from rusting.

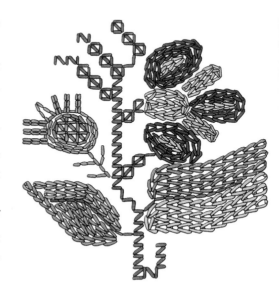

ABILITY LEVEL: Intermediate

SIZE OF FINISHED PINCUSHION:
19.5 x 14 cm/7½ x 5½in

SIZE OF MOTIF:
3 x 2.5 cm/1¼ x 1in

**STRANDED COTTON/
EMBROIDERY FLOSS:** 2 strands

NEEDLE SIZE: 8

FABRIC:
Two pieces 22.5 x 17 cm/9 x 7in
fine cream cotton or linen,

or Zweigart 36-count Edinborough 3217 (Linen, Col no 101), or Charles Craft 32-count Real Irish Linen (Col "Cream" or "Tea Dyed").

TO EMBROIDER AND MAKE UP
1 Embroider motifs (reduce pattern to 50%) on the two pieces of material. When finished, press the material so that it is square and even.

2 Place the two pieces right sides together. Allowing a 1.5 cm/⅝in seam, machine-stitch all the way around, leaving a 5 cm/2in gap on one of the short sides.

3 Turn the pincushion right side out and press. Stuff it, and when completely filled, slipstitch the opening closed.

COLOURS AND STITCHES:

			DMC	Anchor
■	⅋	ⓜ	349	46
▢		ⓜ	703	243
▨		ⓜ	3345	217
▨		ⓜ	731	844
▢		ⓜ	891	11
▢		⅋	402	313
■		⅋	938	380

RIGHT   The same motif is repeated all over the cushion, with varying colours on the flowers.
ABOVE   Closely spaced rows of chain stitch give solid areas of colour and a pleasing texture.

Heart-motif cushion

This wonderful piece of cross stitch is a very good example of symbolic embroidery. It uses geometric hearts and stylized carnations – both are symbols of fertility and love. Equally, the repetitive patterns are good examples of the way embroidery has evolved over the centuries, from literal images to figurative symbols, as described in the introduction to this book.

The embroidered material was purchased in London, England from a dealer in antique textiles. It is particularly treasured for its crudely handloomed linen, as well as for the fading reddish pink of the cotton and the naïve charm of the pattern. It was made into a cushion cover so that it could be used and appreciated on a daily basis, and luckily it is a hardy piece that has survived the chaos of family life.

It is not known what this embroidery was originally intended for. It might well have been a practice piece made by a young girl. Although its provenance is uncertain, its charm and decorative value are not, and with the careful plotting required in counted work, it will be rewarding to complete.

ABOVE Stylized hearts are especially effective in cross stitch.
LEFT Although this original cover fits a rectangular cushion, the length of the embroidered panel can be adjusted to fit any size.

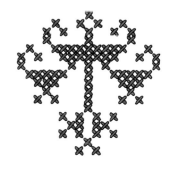

ABILITY LEVEL: Intermediate

SIZE OF FINISHED CUSHION:
48 x 44 cm/19 x 17½in

**WIDTH OF EMBROIDERED
AREA:** 29 cm/11½in (patterns are
actual size).

**NUMBER OF STITCHES PER
2.5 CM (1IN):** 11

**STRANDED
COTTON/EMBROIDERY FLOSS:**
6 strands

NEEDLE SIZE: 5

FABRIC:
One piece 51 x 47 cm/
20 x 18½in for embroidery;
another piece 51 x 55 cm/20 x
22in for cushion back, in cream
cotton or linen, or Zweigart 18-
count Fine Aida 3793 (Cotton,
Col no 400), or Charles Craft
18-count cross-stitch fabric
(Col "Natural" or "Fiddler's").
Two 1.5 cm/⅝in matching
buttons.

TO MAKE UP

1 Press the embroidered piece so
that it is square and even.

2 Cut the other piece of material
in two, going from shorter side
to shorter side (to make an opening
down the centre back of the
cushion). On each side of the
centre cut, turn over to the
wrong side 1 cm/⅜in, then another
2 cm/¾in to make a hem. Pin,
press and machine-stitch.

3 Along one of the hems, measure
in 17.5 cm/7in from each raw edge.
Make a buttonhole, at right
angles to the hem, at each point.
Lap that hem over the other and
sew on the buttons.

4 Place the embroidered material
over the buttoned back, right sides
together, and pin around four sides,
allowing a 1.5 cm/⅝in seam.
Machine-stitch, and finish the
raw edges to prevent fraying.

5 Undo the buttons, turn the cover
right side out and insert the cushion.

COLOURS AND STITCHES:

		DMC	Anchor
■	✕	321	47

Geometric cushion

This intricately embroidered piece was bought from an antique textile dealer in London, England. However, it is not English but most probably Eastern European – or even Russian. I chose it because it has a naïve, stylized look that is very appealing in antique embroidery.

The cushion cover itself has been made from a natural hand-loomed linen that is oatmeal-coloured, which seems to have some irregularities in its weave.

The type of background cloth used for many of the projects featured in this book is often very important to the quality and style of the piece, and that is certainly true of this project. Great care should be taken to find the right cloth on which to embroider – there would be nothing worse than putting a great deal of effort into something where the material subsequently proves to be too insubstantial or totally unsuitable for cleaning. Nevertheless, it need not always be a modern or new cloth that you choose – if you find

an antique piece of plain linen, imagine how pretty it could look embroidered.

This particular design is filled with symbolic patterns which have evolved over the centuries from realistic representations into more geometric shapes. There are flowers and outlined leaves and buds, within alternating borders of red and green.

They are stitched in a dense, half-cross stitch, quite similar to the sort of stitch used in tapestry work or needlepoint. The direction of the stitches alternates, creating a pleasing texture that seems to intensify the effect of the design.

Because of the intricate nature of the stitchery, as well as the sheer volume of work involved, this project is really only recommended for the very experienced embroiderer. This is particularly relevant if you are using an uneven fabric, as the irregularities of the woven threads make the spacing and sizing of the stitches more demanding.

RIGHT The use of alternating colours on this cushion, red and blue flowers within red and green borders, is a clever touch.
ABOVE The main line of pattern features a large flower motif, edged on each side by a plainer border.

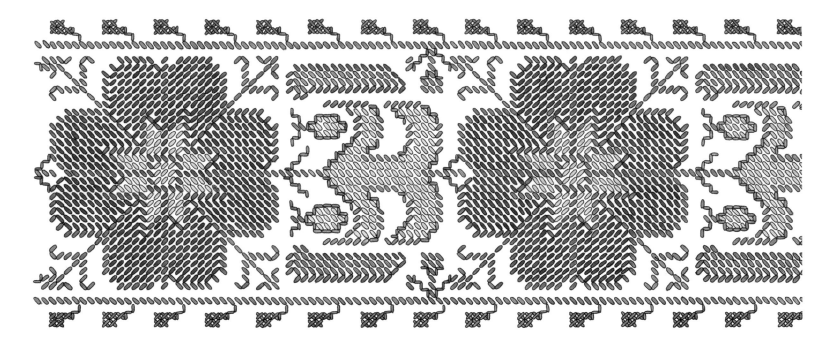

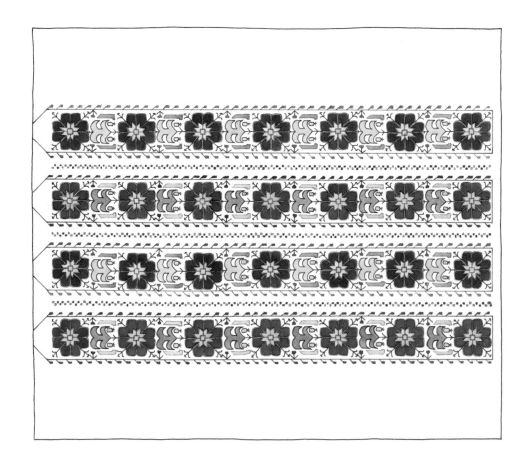

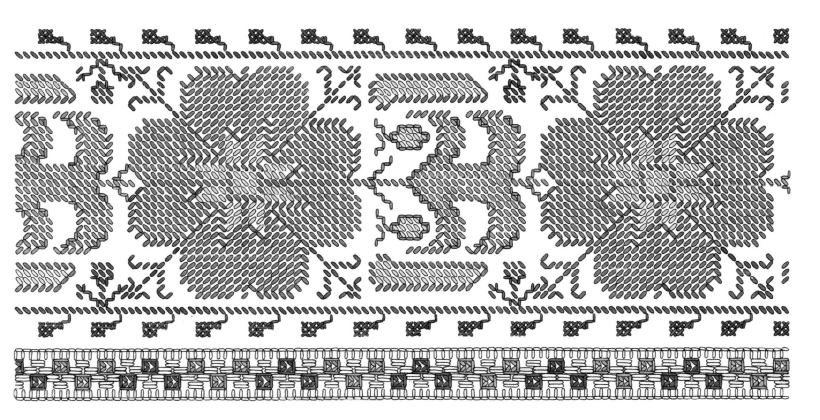

ABILITY LEVEL: Advanced

SIZE OF FINISHED CUSHION:
52 x 46 cm/20½ x 18in

**SIZE OF FINISHED STITCHED
AREA:** 51 x 32.5 cm/20 x 13in
(reduce patterns to 83%).

**STRANDED COTTON/
EMBROIDERY FLOSS:** 4 strands

NEEDLE SIZE: 5

FABRIC:
Two pieces 55 x 49 cm/22 x 19½in
natural-coloured linen or Zweigart
28-count Quaker Cloth 3993

(Linen/Cotton, Col no 309),
or Charles Craft 28-count Real
Irish Linen (Col "Tea Dyed").
2.2 m x 2.5 cm/2½yd x 1in-wide
matching cream cotton lace.

TO MAKE UP
1 Press the embroidered piece so
that it is square and even.

2 Place the two pieces, right sides
together, and pin around two long
sides and one short side, allowing a
1.5 cm/⅝in seam all around.
Machine-stitch, leaving a gap at one
end to insert the cushion.

3 Turn the cushion cover right side

out, insert the cushion, and slipstitch
the opening closed.

4 Pin lace around the edge of the
cushion cover and stitch in place.

COLOURS AND STITCHES:

		DMC	Anchor
		815	1006
		825	979
		612	832
		610	898
		726	297
		832	907
		945	367
		991	879
		352	9

Index

Acknowledgements

Many thanks to the following people who helped with the quest for finding examples of antique needlework: Fiona King at Charleville Gallery, Mariane Goder, Angel Hughes at Tobias and the Angel, Robert and Josyane Young at Robert Young Antiques, Gretchen at The Lacquer Chest, Katerina Mannerfelt at the Blue Door, and Marylin Garrow. Thanks also to Hänsi Schneider, Molly McKinley, Carol Glasser, Michael and Sally Burrows, Christina Probert-Jones, Roderick and Gillie James, Martin Durham and Gill Pratt.

Many thanks to: David Montgomery for his lovely photographs and his positive attitude; Jacqui Small and Larraine Shamwana, our calm and professional art directors, Ingunn Jensen for all her good work on the layouts, and Margot Richardson, a thorough editor.

London, March 1995.